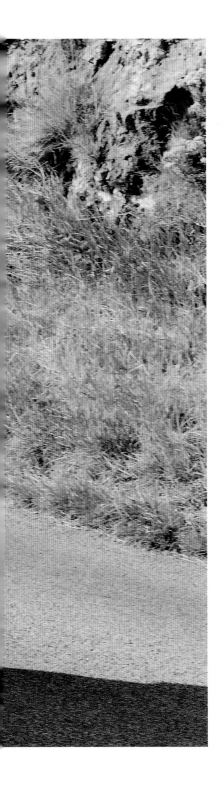

MOTORCYCLE TOURING

BIBLE

FRED RAU

motorbooks

First published in 2010 by MBI Publishing Company LLC and Motorbooks, an imprint of MBI Publishing Company, 400 First Avenue North, Suite 300, Minneapolis, MN, 55401 USA

The information in this book is true and complete to the best of our knowledge. All recommendations are made without any guarantee on the part of the author or Publisher, who also disclaim any liability incurred in connection with the use of this data or specific details.

We recognize, further, that some words, model names, and designations mentioned herein are the property of the trademark holder. We use them for identification purposes only. This is not an official publication.

MBI Publishing Company titles are also available at discounts in bulk quantity for industrial or sales-promotional use. For details write to Special Sales Manager at MBI Publishing Company, 400 First Avenue North, Suite 300, Minneapolis, MN, 55401 USA

ISBN-13: 978-0-7603-3741-7

Editor: Darwin Holmstrom
Design Manager: Kou Lor
Layout by: John Sticha
Cover designed by: Pauline M. Molinari

Printed in China

About the Author
Fred Rau has been a professional motorcycle journalist for more than 35 years, serving as the editor of *Wing World*, the magazine for the Gold Wing Riders Association, and as the managing editor of *Road Rider*. In 1991 he co-founded *Motorcycle Consumer News*. He has ridden well over 1 million miles on all types of motorcycles and currently operates Fred Rau Adventure Tours. He lives in Mission Viejo, California.

On the front cover: *Illustration by Veronica Hill*

Contents

Dedication

To my wife, Cherrie, who nagged me onto my first motorcycle, and without whose constant encouragement and support this book would have never been written.

Acknowledgments

The Author wishes to thank:

Chaparral Motorsports of San Bernardino, California (chaparraledealership.com), for the use of their facilities and extensive inventory for many of the product photos used in this book.

Streetmasters Motorcycle Workshops of Corona, California (streetmasters.info), for allowing me to photograph several of their training classes at Willow Springs Motorsports Park.

Roy Oliemuller, Rob Mitchell, and all the other great folks at BMW of North America, who kindly loaned me new motorcycles for many of my travels over the years in researching this book.

Introduction

Not too long ago, I read an amazing statistic that claimed over 70 percent of all Americans had never traveled beyond the borders of their home state, and that almost 50 percent had never been more than 100 miles from the place where they were born. To someone like me—or perhaps I should say "us," since you're reading this book—this seems almost unbelievable. And yet, even though I consider myself an avid traveler, I have at least a half-dozen motorcycling friends whose adventures and accumulated mileage make me look like a homebody.

I've often wondered if the traveling bug came to me by way of motorcycling, or if the reverse is true. Did I get into motorcycling because I like to travel, or do I like to travel because I'm into motorcycling?

My first traveling adventures came to me by way of my grandparents and had nothing to do with two-wheelers. Though my parents were exactly the kind of stay-at-homes portrayed in the statistics, my grandparents did a lot of traveling in their later years, and luckily for me, they didn't mind taking their grandson along. From the backseat of Grandpa's Buick, I got to see the great American Southwest of Colorado, New Mexico, and Arizona when I was only 12 years old, and I credit that trip as the reason I left Missouri and moved out west just as soon as I was old enough to leave home.

From that point on, I traveled in my car every chance I got, until meeting and marrying my wife, Cherrie, who introduced me to motorcycles. After that the two of us began

This blurry old photo is of me and my first new motorcycle, a 1974 Kawasaki K100. Though it had most of the attributes of a dirt bike (long-throw suspension, knobby tires, high fenders), it was equipped with turn signals and such to make it street legal. This is what we would today call a "dual-sport," though back then most of us called them "combination bikes." It had no backseat, but my wife wanted to ride, so we bungied a beach towel onto the rear fender and made her a seat! I can't imagine being that stupid, but obviously I was.

exploring the world on motorcycles, and still haven't stopped almost 40 years later. In fact, looking back, I see our mileage has increased almost every year. So maybe it's a combination of my grandparents and my wife who are to blame for my wanderlust?

Then again, what about genetics? Is it in my blood? A genealogical survey my mother had taken of our family some years back would seem to add credence to that theory. Going back as far as the fifteenth century, it seems I come from a long line of ship's captains and various other seafarers, including a few nefarious "privateers," which is a nice way of saying "pirates." And more than a few of my ancestors took up flying—one uncle flew with Chenault's "Flying Tigers" in Burma, and another flew with the RAF during the Battle of Britain. One of my grandfathers traveled the world for a mining company, seeking mineral deposits in out-of-the-way places, and the other surveyed railroad routes through previously untraveled territories.

The common thread, it seems, is that none of them stayed put in any one place for very long, and most developed some kind of bond with whatever form of transportation could get them the farthest and the fastest

As I was learning that I enjoyed longer, paved rides, and since Cherrie seemed determined to accompany me, in 1977 we upgraded to a Honda CB750K. This was one of the largest and most powerful bikes in the world at the time, and with our camping gear strapped to the sissybar, we toured all over the American Southwest without any problems.

After dozens of weekend and day trips, in 1985 we took off on a three-week tour through Colorado, Utah, California, and New Mexico. Even the Wing's spacious luggage couldn't carry everything we thought we needed, so the camping gear was strapped over the trunk, obviously overloading the bike, but we didn't know any better at the time. Look at what I considered proper riding gear at the time!

at the time—ships, planes, trains, and of course motorcycles: the man I'm named for, my grandfather Fred Rau Senior, once rode a 1914 Excelsior Super Ace motorcycle from Atchison, Kansas, to San Diego, California, in 1917—before there were paved roads on the route, or, for that matter, any roads at all for large portions. So it would seem I have a pretty solid hereditary claim to my nomadic lifestyle.

These days I find I can't stay in one place for more than about two weeks at a stretch without coming down with a bad case of cabin fever. My wife has learned to recognize the symptoms, and will sometimes say,

"You're getting cranky—time to go for a ride somewhere." From what I've heard from many of my riding friends, most of them are the same way. At the far end of the spectrum are people like Greg Frazier and Mike Kneebone, to whom riding coast-to-coast is a "warmup ride" for more serious adventures.

Of course, there are also a large number of motorcyclists who never tour at all. And I'm not talking about those who have jobs or family responsibilities that limit them to weekend rides or a once-a-year vacation trek to Sturgis, Daytona, Americade, or some other destination. I'm talking about those who simply have no desire to travel on their bikes. People who trailer their bikes to the track and run around in circles all day, or to a motorcycle rally where they can putt up and down the main street for an hour or two. That kind of motorcycling makes no sense to me, but I guess it does to them, and I shouldn't give them a hard time about it. Their concept of motorcycling is different from mine. Not better or worse—just different. But I have trouble relating with such riders, and I suppose I always will.

To me, the perfect motorcycling experience is getting up every morning knowing I'll be riding all day, on roads and through scenery I've never seen before, to a destination where I've never been, and with the knowledge that I'll be doing the same thing again tomorrow, and the next day, and the next, and so on. If heaven exists, for me it will be just like this.

To a certain extent, this book is for others who feel the same way. But for the most part, it's for riders who have only been bitten by the touring bug fairly recently—say within the past couple of years. These riders are just beginning what to me and so many others has been a lifelong journey. What I want to share with them is some of the knowledge I've gained along the way, to accelerate and enhance their own touring experience.

I hope I succeed.

Fred Rau Senior, the man I was named for, aboard his 1914 Excelsior Super Ace in 1917. Grandpa was one of the world's first long-distance touring riders, piloting this bike from Atchison, Kansas, to Monterey, California, and back again in July of 1917. Almost exactly 90 years later, I would attempt to duplicate his route.

Chapter 1

What Is Motorcycle Touring?

Ask 20 different motorcyclists what makes a motorcycle tour, and you're likely to get at least 20 different answers. And if there is one important thing I want you to remember as you're reading this book, it's that virtually no definition of the term is any more correct than the others. That's perhaps the ultimate beauty of this endeavor (or "pastime," or "sport," or whatever you like to call it)—

motorcycle touring comes in a myriad of forms, each with its own set of challenges and pleasures. To give the book a sense of order, I've set some guidelines based strictly on my own opinions and experiences, just so we all know what we're talking about here.

First, let's talk about the different kinds of motorcycle travelers. The most common distinctions among those who tour on two wheels can be expressed by these categories: time and distance and bike and riding style.

Day trips, either alone or with a partner, are the obvious first step when getting into motorcycle touring. Some people will be content with this sort of touring and never feel the need for anything else, but for a large percentage of us, it will only whet our appetites for more. Weekenders with a few friends are the next step up the touring ladder. On a weekend trip, you're seldom so far away from home that minor problems can't be put off until your return, and you have friends with you to help out, if needed. Weekenders allow you to experiment with things like packing techniques, finding out what you really need, and learning what is non-essential. Eventually, of course, the ultimate dream of almost any touring motorcyclist is the extended tour to a foreign land—the more exotic, the better. But before attempting a ride of this magnitude, there is much you need to learn, grasshopper. Your progression from Daytripper to Experienced Foreign Traveler is what this book is all about.

For some people, "sport" is what riding is all about, even when they're touring, and a regular sport-tourer is too much of a compromise. Such folks will take their pure sport bike, attach whatever kind of luggage they can, and hit the road. My only advice to those people is to at least do it the way the pretty redhead on the Kawasaki ZRX in the top photo did, and get throw-over saddlebags and a tankbag for your gear. This keeps your packing weight centered and low on the bike and has the least negative effect on your bike's handling. The couple on the other bike opted to carry all their gear on the luggage rack and sissybar, high up and behind the rear axle. This effectively leverages weight off the front axle, reducing traction for cornering and braking. Not a very good idea.

Defining a Tour by Time and Distance

How long do you need to be on the road before a ride becomes a tour? Does a single, overnight stay away from home qualify? And for that matter, how far do you need to ride? To some people, riding 100 miles is a long trip. To others, that's a rough indicator of a good time to stop for breakfast. As I said before, ask 20 riders and you'll probably get 20 or more opinions. For the sake of clarity, I'll make up some arbitrary categories and use them through the ensuing chapters.

Day Trips

Though many might not consider a day trip worthy of being called a tour, to beginning tour riders it's a starting point that will eventually lead to bigger and better things. For that reason, we'll touch on day trips occasionally here, though for the most part the things we'll be discussing won't apply. I consider a day trip to be any ride that starts and ends in the same place on the same day.

Day trips are not only fun, but also serve a very useful purpose as tune-ups

Some people like to travel to big motorcycle gatherings, like Sturgis, and hang out for a week. To me, such events are way too crowded and seem to have little to do with actually riding motorcycles. I don't mind stopping off for a day, but I'm usually back on the road within 24 hours.

Before you consider going it alone on a week-long or longer tour, you might want to consider taking an organized tour with a club or a professional tour operator. Again, if problems come up, you're not alone.

for longer rides. It's only through a succession of day trips that we learn such important things as how far the bike will go on a tank of gas, how warm those gloves really are, which suspension settings work best, or any number of other pieces of useful information that will become invaluable on longer rides, such as my own personal favorite: "How far can my passenger go between restroom stops?"

Weekenders

A "weekender" is pretty self-explanatory: it's a ride that starts on Friday or Saturday and ends when you get back home on Sunday. Of course, sometimes we finish our trip on Monday afternoon, to take advantage of a long holiday weekend. So these extended weekends might actually involve as many as three nights and four days on the road. Like the day trips, weekenders can serve as shakedown tours that provide us with valuable experience and insight that will serve us well on longer tours, particularly when it comes to things like packing. Weekenders are also very useful for breaking in new equipment like helmets, boots, jackets, and of course motorcycles.

> **For our purposes here, consider a "tour" to be a ride that's longer than three nights, up to and including as many as two weeks on the road.**

Tours

For our purposes here, consider a "tour" to be a ride that's longer than three nights, up to and including as many as two weeks on the road. These are the types of rides that most of us live for, whether we take them once every couple of years or as often as every few months. It's this kind of tour that is the primary focus of this book.

In reality, it's probably safe to say that a tour could run from 500 miles to 5,000 miles or more; in this book, we will limit them to approximately 3,000 miles and two weeks of traveling. Beyond that, we will be referring to …

Extended Tours

For me and many others, an "extended tour" is the ultimate motorcycling experience, involving either a ride that lasts more than two weeks, one that takes us to exotic, foreign locations, or a combination of both. For most riders, extended tours are pretty much once-in-a-lifetime (or at least once-in-a-decade) experiences.

Those riders lucky enough to have the time and financial wherewithal to go on more than three such tours in their life probably only comprise about 10 percent of all touring riders. That being the case, we want to do everything in our power to prepare for the experience, so as to minimize the chances that something will go wrong and spoil a trip of a lifetime. That, my friends, is exactly what this book is all about.

Defining a Tour by Bike and Riding Style

This may be the most difficult and contentious type of classification to make. Millions of words have been written defining the different types of motorcycle touring, and no clear consensus has ever been reached. But at least it keeps those motorcycle Internet chat rooms buzzing.

Here are the categories I use:

Sport-Touring

Touring conducted on a sport bike such as a Yamaha R1, Ducati 1198, Suzuki GSX-R 750, or a Buell XB12S, or a specialized sport-touring bike such as the Honda ST1300, Yamaha FJR1300, Kawasaki Concours, BMW RT or GT, and too many others to list. Those who tour on sport bikes mostly use soft-sided, detachable luggage, or specialized "tour packs" that fit on the backseat.

Sport-touring is most commonly defined by bikes like this Honda ST1300—built by the manufacturer as touring machines, but with many of the handling and power characteristics of a sport bike. Note the integrated fairing, detachable hard luggage, and luggage rack behind the seat. Sport-touring bikes like the Yamaha FJR and BMW RT almost always have extended-range fuel tanks, and windshields that are adjustable for either sport or touring conditions.

The Honda Gold Wing has pretty much stood at the top of the heap for luxury touring bikes for over a quarter-century. Though there are other good luxury tourers, like the BMW LT and even the Harley-Davidson Electra Glide, none has ever quite matched the Wing's combination of power, performance, and luxury amenities.

Specialized sport-touring bikes, such as those mentioned above, all have factory-installed (yet still detachable) hard saddlebags and optional trunks.

For the most part, sport-tourers are more concerned with the performance aspects of their mounts than with creature comforts. For example, sport-touring riders would probably be more apt to spend money on upgrading suspension or exhaust (for better handling or more power) than they would on adding a satellite radio or communications system. Not to say that sport-tourers don't buy these things, only that such equipment is a usually a lower priority for them.

I've also found that sport-touring riders, among all touring riders, seem the most cognizant of the need for proper riding gear and advanced rider training. Some people will take exception to this, but please remember it's only a generalization and certainly not meant to imply other riders never wear proper gear or engage in advanced training. Still, I'll stand by my assessment that within the sport-touring community, there is a culture and mindset that prizes skill, training, and safety more than just about any other segment of the motorcycling community.

Luxury Touring
Over the years, as bikes got larger and more complex, a new segment of motorcycle touring began to evolve: luxury touring. I consider a luxury touring bike one

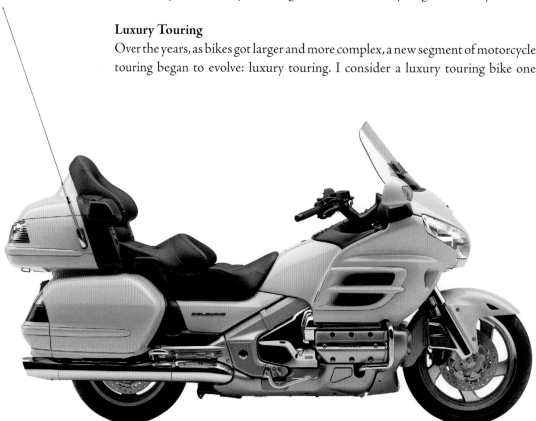

with OEM (original equipment manufacturer) luggage, fairing, and windshield, and at least several of the following accessory options: stereo, intercom, a global positioning system (GPS), cruise control, heated seats or handgrips, two-way radio, and so on. Currently, the most common bikes in this genre are the Honda Gold Wing, the Harley-Davidson Electra Glide and Road Glide, the Victory Vision, and the BMW LT series. There are bikes that blur the line between classes, but we need not concern ourselves too much with that, as all of these groupings are merely generalizations.

Riders of luxury touring bikes may not be quite as into performance as their sport-touring counterparts, but for the most part they ride just as much and just as far (if not farther). Luxury tourers are also usually a bit more destination-oriented than route-oriented, and are much more likely to be found riding two-up.

Cruiser Touring

In an odd way, cruiser touring is probably both the oldest and the newest class of motorcycle touring. The original touring riders often rode bikes that we would consider cruisers today (they were just plain old motorcycles back then), and they used these bikes for everything, from commuting to work to cross-country touring.

In the past decade, the fastest-growing segment of touring has probably been cruiser-touring, fueled by bikes like this Yamaha Royal Star Tour Deluxe. Some of these cruiser-tourers blur the line for luxury touring with their comfort and amenities, but none really come close to the power and handling of bikes like the Wing or the BMW LT. Cruiser-tourers are more about a relaxed touring style, which is exactly what many people are looking for.

The newer crop of cruiser tourers are mostly made up of riders who started riding cruisers for their relaxed riding style and then expanded their horizons to something beyond the weekend boulevard cruise, for which the style was named. Cruisers are generally considered to be those bikes with a more feet-forward riding position and a semi-stretched frame and/or somewhat extended front fork.

Cruisers have low ground clearance and seat heights, which often makes them ideal for shorter riders. For the most part, cruiser designers emphasize styling rather than performance. Some of that has started to change lately, though, with some of the newer cruisers sporting more powerful engines and improved suspensions, which has improved their capabilities for touring. Recognizing the trend, most manufacturers now offer special touring versions of their cruiser models, equipped with windshields and hard saddlebags, though the bags are usually disguised to look like leather throw-overs so as not to ruin the original cruiser look.

> The original touring riders often rode bikes that we would consider cruisers today (they were just plain old motorcycles back then), and they used these bikes for everything, from commuting to work to cross-country touring.

Even though a fair-sized segment of cruiser riders have started touring, many of them tend to ride considerably shorter distances than luxury or sport-touring riders. When they do take challenging secondary routes, they tend to ride at a more sedate pace than do sport-touring and even luxury touring riders. That's entirely understandable, as most cruiser bikes have abbreviated suspensions, wider turning radii, and less power than other touring bikes, making them a challenge to handle on narrow, tight roads. Cruiser touring is more about relaxing and taking it easy than the somewhat frenetic world of sport-touring, or even the long-haul tendencies of luxury touring.

Scooter Touring

This class should be pretty much self-explanatory: it's simply those who like to tour on scooters rather than regular motorcycles. Scooter touring has been around for as long as scooters have existed, and was fairly popular in Europe during the 1950s and 1960s. But it never really started to catch on here in the U.S. until Japanese manufacturers began making larger-displacement scooters in the 1990s. The reason was simple: nearly all scooters were illegal on the

Also growing in popularity are the newer touring scooters. This latest generation of scooters, like the Suzuki Burgman (pictured) and the Honda Silver Wing, have the power to cruise at highway speeds, even with luggage and two riders.

highways of America, not to mention being downright dangerous, because they lacked the power and speed to keep up with traffic. However, nowadays, with scooters like the Honda Silver Wing and the Suzuki Burgman, we now have scooters with performance specs that would easily rival a full-sized motorcycle made just a couple of decades ago. With 400cc and 650cc engines, much improved suspensions, and oversized trunks and luggage racks, this new generation of scooters has proven itself perfectly capable of touring.

For the most part, scooter touring people are of, shall we say . . . advancing years, but it certainly doesn't seem to keep them from hitting the roads, and for some fairly long distances. Never count out the scooter touring crowd.

Endurance and Dual-Sport (Adventure) Touring

For the purposes of this book, we won't include these classes in our conversations about motorcycle touring. It's enough to say that endurance tourers are riders who make it their business to rack up as many miles as possible in as short a timespan as possible. It's almost a cult thing, represented primarily by the Iron Butt Association, which sanctions and organizes special events for these mileage slaves. They're definitely a breed apart, fanatically dedicated riders

Dual-sport, or "adventure" touring, like scooter touring, isn't a large part of the touring market, but the aficionados of this niche are avid and enthusiastic. They like to point out, and rightfully so, that 75 percent of the world's roads aren't paved—why should you deprive yourself of them?

In addition to dirt and gravel "improved" roads, full-bore adventure touring also means getting completely off the road wherever possible, on bikes specifically designed for such riding. The milder form of this sport is usually referred to as dual-sporting, and involves bikes like the Kawasaki KLR, Suzuki V-Strom, and a favorite of mine, the BMW F650GS (pictured here in the Swiss Alps). These bikes are biased more toward riding on regular, paved roads, but are also designed with high ground clearance and extended suspensions that are well-suited for dirt roads, so long as you don't get into anything too gnarly. Dual-sport machines are particularly useful for touring in developing countries, where the roads are much narrower and twistier than the ones we're used to in North America. For example, though I might tour the U.S. on a Gold Wing, I would never ride it in the Austrian Alps or Italian Dolomites, where the nature of the roadways confines you almost exclusively to speeds around 45 mph, on roads so narrow that you might have to pull onto the shoulder for vehicles coming the other way. In these situations, a big touring bike is more of a liability than an asset.

who certainly have no need of my advice about motorcycle touring, and so won't be covered in this book.

Dual-sport, also called "adventure" touring, has become increasingly popular in the U.S. over the past decade or so, to the point that virtually every motorcycle manufacturer now has several new models specifically designed for the class. Basically, dual-sport touring differs from other kinds of motorcycle touring because it involves getting off paved roads. Dual-sport bikes are hybrids of dirt bikes and street bikes, and while not ideal for going entirely off-road are well designed for dirt, gravel, and what we loosely call "unimproved" roadways.

Like dirt bikes, dual-sports require very high ground clearance, extended rough-duty suspensions, long-range fuel tanks, semi-knobby tires, and plenty of low-end torque. Unfortunately most of those qualities work against the bike when it's on pavement, but it's still remarkable how well the manufacturers have managed to meld the two classes into a single bike.

The bottom line is that dual-sport or adventure touring is in a class by itself, with a whole new set of parameters and equipment that don't really cross over into the other touring disciplines, and so will be left out of our *Touring Bible*. In truth, someone could easily do an entire book just about adventure touring, to the exclusion of all else—not to mention the fact that I've only been dual-sporting three times in my life, and thus am far from an expert on the subject.

Top: On the far edge of the touring spectrum we have the endurance, or "iron butt" riders. These mileage slaves have no concern except traveling farther than anyone else, in less time. The sport has gained quite a cult following, like any other extreme sport, and spawned its own sub-culture of custom bikes, like this highly modified BMW RTP (P for "police model"). Note the six extra driving lights for riding 24-hour days; the twin GPS units, backed up by a full-sized laptop for navigation; the satellite antennas; ice tracker; and on the luggage rack, an extended-range fuel cell. Bikes like this are most commonly used to compete in events like the International Iron Butt Rally, where the rider must complete 11,000 miles in 11 days just to qualify for a finisher's plaque. Winning the rally takes more . . . much more. Two photos below: Honda now offers a navigation system for its Gold Wing.

Fairings and the Vetter Legacy

A curve that has no breaks in it is called "continuous" by mathematicians; likewise, a curve that has no sharp corners in it is called "smooth" by mathematicians. Smooth means the first derivative of the curve is continuous. At any given point, a curve has a radius of curvature. If there are no sudden jumps in the radius of curvature, the curve is called "fair." A fair curve has a continuous second derivative. Early on in aircraft design, it was learned that turbulent flow always starts at a point on the skin where the curve has an abrupt change in the radius of curvature—that is, a point where the curve is not fair, or a point where the second derivative is discontinuous. So, you can't just stick a wing onto an airplane fuselage—the sharp corner where they meet is not even smooth, much less fair. Designers soon found they had to locate places like this on the aircraft skin and cover them with some smoothly curved sheet metal. These pieces of sheet metal are called "fairings."

Craig Vetter (2002): "I did not invent the motorcycle fairing. Three brands were known to us in the 1960s. The English Avon and Butler brands were 'dolphin-style' frame-mounted fairings. They were neat looking but not suitable to the American riding style of sitting upright with high, wide handlebars. The American brand best known was the Wixom, made by Dean and Stan Wixom. Wixom fairings were handlebar-mounted and made for the American riding stance, and were popular on BMWs. The current Harley 'Batwing' fairing is a derivative.

My first fairing, the Series 1000, was like an English fairing, but made wider for American handlebars. My design was also much simpler. Mine was the first fairing that was not more trouble than it was worth. In addition, I was able to figure out how to make it light and inexpensive, and to market it."

Craig Vetter was studying product design at the University of Illinois in the early 1960s when he saw a fellow student riding a Honda 50 Cub. Vetter was attracted to the quiet and efficient Japanese motorcycle, and soon became an avid motorcyclist. A friend of Craig's named Duane Anderson rode his Yamaha 250 from Illinois to Colorado the summer after graduation to attend the Aspen Design Conference. Anderson's trip inspired Vetter to make the same trip the next year on his Yamaha 305, but he found riding on the open road a tiring experience. Forced to ride hunched forward, with eyes squinted against the wind blast, at one point in the middle of Kansas, Vetter settled in close behind a truck for relief.

"Suddenly I could enjoy the ride," Vetter recalls. "I was able to sit up and open my eyes and enjoy my surroundings. It was then I realized I wanted some sort of wind protection."

Vetter began work on making his own fairing in the fall of 1966 by wheeling his Yamaha into his living room, where he had drilled eyebolts into the floor so he could strap the bike down. He fashioned his first fairing patterns from home insulation foam. He used a carpenter's square to keep the first fairing even on both sides, but later found that the floor in his living room had sagged, and the design was slightly crooked. After having one of his prototypes dissolve in a rainstorm, he enlisted boat-shop owner Ray Diskin to give him a 15-minute crash course on resin mixing and laminating, but quickly found that

he did not like working with fiberglass and arranged for Diskin to make the fairing from the original mold. On November 2, 1967, Vetter mounted his new fairing on his Yamaha (he was so excited he couldn't wait for a windshield to mount it on) and took a test ride.

A friend bought that first fairing, and Vetter knew there was a potential market for his creation. His first aftermarket, bolt-on motorcycle fairing sold for about $100, and Craig only sold around 100 of the somewhat ungainly-looking items, but the die was cast. Basically, a "fairing" was nothing more complex than a molded fiberglass shell that attached to the front of a motorcycle, improving both the bike's aerodynamic and the rider's protection from the elements. Fairings certainly weren't a new idea, considering that Ernst Henne had set a world land speed record on a fully-faired BMW in 1937, but they were considered to be strictly for racing, and I don't believe anyone sold them as standard equipment on any bike in the world. Besides, this was before plastics, and most of those early efforts were custom-fashioned from wood or metal, heavy and expensive to produce.

But with a mass-produced, inexpensive, and lightweight Vetter fairing attached to the bike, riders now found they could ride farther, faster, and in greater comfort than ever before in history.

In 1971, Vetter refined his design into the "Windjammer" series, and things exploded. In one year, 10,000 Windjammers were sold. In 1973 the Windjammer II sold 25,000 units, and 1974 saw the Windjammer III reach sales of 75,000. By 1977, Craig had further refined his design into the all-new Windjammer SS, which would reach a sales volume of over 150,000 units, at which point the motorcycle industry began to sit up and take notice.

Though a small percentage of motorcyclists had always toured on their bikes, for most riders it simply wasn't an option. Bikes were too unreliable and uncomfortable. The rider's exposure to the

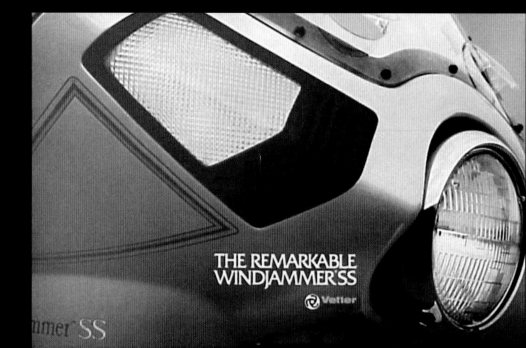

ments was just a bit too much for most people to tolerate. Perhaps by the sheer luck of having exactly the right product at exactly the right time in history, Vetter would change that attitude completely. The Japanese "Big Four" (Honda, Suzuki, Kawasaki, and Yamaha) were just starting to dominate the U.S. motorcycle market, and doing so with ever larger, more powerful, and considerably more reliable machines than American riders had ever seen—and because of those qualities, the owners started to ride them farther and farther. The only issue remaining to be addressed was rider comfort, and Craig Vetter jumped into that gap with both feet.

Though the Vetter fairings were made for and used on virtually every make and model of motorcycle produced, the seminal example, and the one that would do the most to change the face of motorcycling, was the one for the Honda Gold Wing. When the GL1000 Gold Wing first arrived in America in 1975, it was not as a touring bike, but as a supersport machine, designed to challenge the Kawasaki KZ 900 (and eventually its KZ 1000 sibling) for streetbike supremacy. The Japanese had no inkling of what lay in store for them, as sales of the big four-cylinder bike started to ramp up. It would be another three years before they even started to catch on that the majority of

Americans were, upon buying flagship supersports, almost immediately retrofitting them with larger, more comfortable saddles, some saddlebags for carrying their luggage, and most importantly, a Vetter fairing for weather protection. The full-on, luxury touring bike had been born.

Craig Vetter, being much quicker on the uptake than the manufacturers, saw that his fairings shipped out as fast as he could build them and realized another gold mine awaited his pickaxe, in the form of lockable, waterproof hard luggage. By 1978, he was building a full line of saddlebags and trunks for the GLs, tastefully designed and painted to be a perfect match for his fairings. In the next three years, he would sell over 100,000 sets of GL luggage, effectively completing the transformation of over 100,000 of Honda's

supersports into the world's first true, full-dress luxury touring bikes.

It took Honda until 1980 to catch up with what was happening, and to begin offering the GL with its own factory-installed and matched fairing and bags, after which the Gold Wing took over total dominance of the heavyweight touring market in the U.S. All of the other manufacturers followed suit, but it's important to note that very quickly the designers began to look beyond just bolting on fairings and bags to completely redesigning their bikes around fixed fairings and/or bags. Though this phenomenon at first was restricted to touring bikes, the concept very quickly spread to sport machines, completely changing the look of sport bikes forever. Today, could we even imagine a CBR, GSX-R, or Ninja

without fully enclosing bodywork and fairing. All thanks to Craig Vetter.

Personally, I feel that Craig is virtually always overlooked when people talk about motorcycle design. Certainly, the accomplishments of those like Massimo Tamburini and David Robb deserve every bit of praise they receive, but in reality, did any of their cutting edge designs have anywhere near as far-reaching an effect on overall motorcycle design as Craig's Windjammers? Today, I can look at dozens, perhaps hundreds of new street motorcycles in the showrooms, and see on each of them, somewhere, a piece, a shape, a shadow of a line that goes back to a mold that Craig Vetter painstakingly shaped on his living room floor with his bare hands, 44 years ago.

We owe the man a debt, or at least a bit more recognition than what he gets.

Chapter 2

Identifying and Prioritizing Your Criteria

Most of us can only afford to own one motorcycle, making it vitally important to choose one that most closely meets our needs. Unfortunately, identifying our personal criteria usually only comes from an extended—and expensive—period of trial and error. Though there's no way I could possibly tell you which bike is best for you, my hope is that through this section, I can at least help you steer around many of the common stumbling blocks you'll encounter as you make this difficult decision.

There are many other factors to be considered in addition to ergonomics in your bike choice. Does it have sufficient fuel range for an extended tour? Is there adequate luggage-carrying capacity? And perhaps most important and also most often overlooked: What is the bike's maximum safe load-carrying capacity? All too often, even a bike sold as a "touring" model doesn't have a frame and suspension setup designed to carry the combined weight of two riders and their luggage. Check the bike's gross vehicle weight rating (GVWR), subtract the actual weight of the bike with a full tank of gas and all the accessories, and see how much is left. If it barely comes up to the combined weight of yourself and a passenger, adding luggage is going to overburden the frame and suspension, and it will result in poor, uncomfortable, and even unsafe handling.

Motorcycle Ergonomics

Take a look at this series of photos, paying particular attention to the angles of the riders' knees, elbows, wrists, and spines. Though it's true that no one bike fits everyone's riding style or body shape and size, you should keep a few basic facts in mind when choosing your own ride. First of all, note the alignment of your ankles and knees. Generally speaking, the closer you can get to a straight up-and-down alignment of the two, the better off you'll be on long days in the saddle. The worst alignment is shown in Photo L, with the feet far in front of the knees. Though this might seem like an ideal, relaxed position for sitting in your recliner at home, on the bike it means that your leg bones and muscles can't support your body weight, leaving the shock of every little bump to run directly through your butt and up your spine. It also makes it virtually impossible for you to shift your weight for cornering maneuvers, or to brace yourself against acceleration forces. The best body alignment for touring is shown in Photos I and K, with the example in I being slightly better because the rider's knees are below the plane of his hips, giving the rider a little bit more leverage.

Though the rider in Photo A has his feet slightly in front of his knees, the position is not nearly as extreme as the one in Photo L, and the rider has compensated somewhat by installing a backrest on his seat for added support. Photo J shows an extreme sport riding posture, which is very good for control, but not so great for long-haul comfort. Photos D and H both show what we would commonly refer to as a sport-touring stance, which is a compromise between comfort and control.

Note the angles and extension on the riders' elbows and wrists. Even some of the riders with good foot and knee placement have positioned themselves so that their arms are fully extended, with no bend to their elbows when riding in a straight line, while even the guy with the horrible leg placement in Photo L has a slight bend to his elbows. The truth is, having your arms fully extended leaves little or no leverage and flexibility for counter-steering. To make the proper inputs for your steering, you'd have to swivel at the shoulders and hips, which isn't a good idea. Try to develop a riding position that allows you to go nearly lock-to-lock with your handlebars without having to twist at the hips and shoulders.

Ultimately you need to decide for yourself which ergonomic setup is best for you. Start with how your body size and shape relates to your bike, then modify the bike as needed with an aftermarket seat, footpegs, handlebars, or relocators.

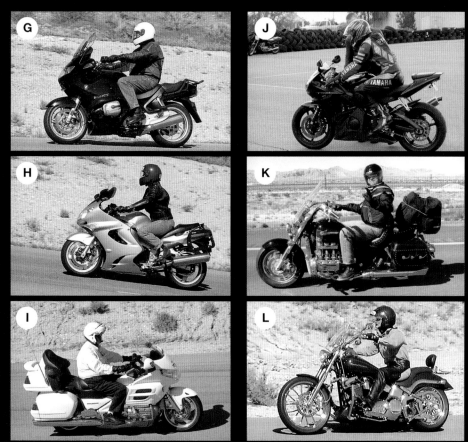

For starters, hopefully you've identified yourself with one of the tourer classes listed in the previous section. That will give you a good starting point on deciding what type of motorcycle is going to come closest to meeting your needs. Naturally no single bike is going to be the best you could have for every riding situation you'll encounter, so you need to set some priorities.

1. Will the Majority of Your Riding Be Solo or Two-up?

You need to predict whether or not you'll be carrying a passenger on a regular basis. You also need to consider whether you'll be riding alone most of the time, commuting back and forth to work or taking day trips alone, or usually be riding with a few friends. Is it perhaps more important that the bike meet your passenger's approval during the weekend and on vacation tours? Remember, as the old maxim goes, "If Momma ain't happy, ain't nobody gonna be happy!"

Sometimes the best roads might be hiding in your own back yard. All you have to do is get off the freeway to discover them.

This great motorcycling road in the middle of Death Valley, called "Artist's Drive," winds through several miles of tight, twisty canyons like this, emerging onto a plateau with fabulous vistas of the valley below. However, it sees almost no traffic at all because it is off the main road and has just one small sign marking its existence. Most tourists bypass it completely, either because they don't know it exists or because it is fairly difficult to negotiate with a four-wheeled vehicle. In fact, motorhomes and trailers are forbidden on this road, and the warning sign probably scares most people away. All of which make it a perfect road for us!

Getting off the beaten path can be rewarding if you're not in any hurry (which you won't be if you've planned your trip wisely). As long as a road has a good, solid surface and is passable, it offers a potentially rewarding route. Just don't do anything foolish—if the road looks like it might become dangerous, turn back. No schedule is worth risking injury or death to keep.

Riding alone, in the United States, I prefer a sport-touring machine like this Honda ST1300. Everything I need packs away nicely in the removable saddlebags. The ergonomics fit me well, the range is terrific (nearly 300 miles on a tank), weather protection is good, and yet it still very much has the feel, power, and handling of a sport machine.

If you place a higher priority on two-up riding, you're naturally going to want a larger, more powerful bike. Not that this is mandatory by any means, but to a certain degree it's just plain old common sense. I once toured the Alpine regions of Austria and Switzerland alone, with practically no luggage, on a 650cc bike, and it was great. But if I'd had my wife along, and a full complement of luggage, I would have strained that poor bike's engine, brakes, and suspension to a dangerous level. Better to upgrade to a 1200cc sport-tourer in that situation, as I did later in New Zealand.

2. Where Do You Plan on Riding It?

Like so many questions, there is no complete and final answer to this, but we can still apply some important generalities. For example, if you live and primarily ride in states such as Florida or Nebraska, you're unlikely to encounter much in the way of tight, twisty mountain roads, are you? Most of your riding will be on fairly wide, open, and for the most part straight roads. In that case, unless you spend a lot of time on a track, you really don't need a bike with the suspension, ground clearance, and lean angles important for someone who lives in the Rocky Mountains. Though the magazine reviews might get you all sweaty with their talk of performance specs, in the long run you're probably going to be a lot happier with a bike designed more for comfort and stability over the long haul.

3. What Type of Ergonomics Do You Want?

Are the ergonomics of the bike better suited for sport riding or for touring? Just because a bike is well built for an hour or two of canyon carving certainly doesn't mean it's ideal for successive 10-hour days in the saddle. There are some riders—usually of the younger, slimmer, and more athletic type—who actually enjoy touring on sport-biased bikes, but they're a small minority. For most of us who tour, long-haul comfort takes priority. Of course, a lot of us will still look for the best power and handling characteristics we can find, but not at the expense of personal comfort. Luckily for us, modern technology has started to blur the lines between sport and sport-touring bikes, and even between sport-touring and luxury touring bikes, so this isn't nearly as tough a decision as it was just a few years ago.

Riding in the Alps, even though two-up, I prefer a smaller, lighter machine. With a higher ground clearance and lighter weight, it is easier to handle through the almost constant barrage of very tight turns. The horsepower of a larger machine is almost a complete waste here, since you rarely reach speeds over about 40 miles per hour or get above third gear. Bottom-end torque is what you really want for pulling you through the turns and up the steep grades. Of course, carrying capacity is very limited, but if you are on a guided tour, with a luggage van service, all you need to carry is a rainsuit and your camera, so a bike like a BMW F650 or Suzuki V-Strom 650 is ideal.

The photo to the right is the Graciosa Trail in Brazil. Here again, as in the Alps, I chose a lightweight 650cc bike, for most of the same reasons. Though the roads in South America are, for the most part, in fairly good repair, you will still encounter many bumps and other irregularities, not to mention things like cobblestone streets in the villages. This again is where the light weight and high ground clearance of bikes like the F650 and V-Strom are of benefit. Try to remember that in most parts of Europe and South America, bigger is not necessarily better. With the exception of the German autobahns, most roads in these parts of the world simply were never designed for high-speed travel, and bikes designed for the American superhighways are out of their element.

4. How Much Luggage Capacity Does It Have?

You'll learn about packing your bike as efficiently as possible in a later section of this book, but before we reach that point, we need to know how much the bike can safely and conveniently hold. Making this determination can be trickier than you might think; simply looking at specification numbers really isn't much help. For starters, nearly all motorcycle manufacturers will give you the capacity of their luggage in liters, which is very deceptive not just because it's a metric measurement, but because it assumes that your luggage is liquid and will fill every available nook and cranny of space. Naturally they do this because it gives them a much bigger number to throw out, but even if used strictly for comparison purposes to other bikes, it really doesn't mean much in terms of actual, usable packing space.

Some saddlebags that look capacious from the outside are actually "cut away" on the inside to make room for an exhaust pipe, battery, or driveline components, leaving very narrow spaces that are difficult to access and are virtually useless. You need to have a hard look at the luggage, or if possible even experiment with packing it, to see what it will really hold. Usually the best answer to this question can be found by talking to someone who already owns the type of bike you're considering.

In addition to the bike's luggage capacity, you should probably take a good look at the type of luggage the bike either comes with or can be equipped with.

Obviously this isn't really a question if you're opting for a full-dress factory touring machine, like the Gold Wing, Electra Glide, or BMW LT, since all those come equipped with hard, locking, permanent saddlebags and trunks (top cases). But if you're considering a sport, sport-touring, or cruiser touring machine, you may have to add "aftermarket" luggage. This can be anything from specially designed nylon packing systems that fit on the backseat or a luggage rack to throw-over saddlebags of leather or nylon. In either case, you need to be cognizant of several things:

- Can it be secured to the bike, so it doesn't disappear while you're in the restaurant or the toilet?
- Is it waterproof?
- Is it lockable?
- And the item most often overlooked: how heavy is it going to be and where will it apply that weight to the bike?

Saddlebags are usually best, as the weight is carried low and either even with or forward of the rear axle. Worst-case are large packs made to fit behind the

This photo was taken on the South Island of New Zealand, near Mount Cook. New Zealand's roads would place it almost in a category of its own, somewhere between North America and Europe. Though there are virtually no multi-lane superhighways, the two-lanes that crisscross the islands are the best-designed and best-maintained roads I have ever encountered. Certainly there are still a lot of very tight, twisty sections through the mountains, but they are also made from an indigenous volcanic rock that provides an incredible coefficient of friction. Here, I always upgrade to a sport-touring bike, such as a BMW R1200RT, Yamaha FJR1300, or Honda ST1300.

Below left: Would you want to pilot a heavyweight touring bike down roads like this, which often amount to little more than goat paths with some token pavement spread over them? Below right: When traveling through some of the most beautiful scenery the world has to offer, less can be more—the less bike you have to worry about, the more you can enjoy the incredible surroundings.

rear seat, on a luggage rack, or on a sissybar. Sure they're convenient and highly functional, but always remember that any weight placed behind and above the rear axle of your bike tends to turn the bike into a lever, like a child's teeter-totter, with the fulcrum at the axle of the rear wheel. That means that every pound you put on the back is leveraging weight *off* your front wheel, unloading your front suspension, and reducing your traction for steering and braking. It can be a dangerous situation, one that won't become evident until the time when you really need that control and braking power, at which time it'll be too late.

For many riders, the best possible scenario is found with the dedicated sport-touring machines like the Honda ST, Yamaha FJR, BMW RT, Kawasaki Concours, and others, which come factory-equipped with hard, waterproof, locking luggage that can also be easily removed and carried into your room at night like normal luggage. Even better, when you're at home or staying several nights in the same location, the bags can be left off the bike entirely, effectively transforming it from a touring mount to an almost pure sport machine.

And finally, I would be remiss if I didn't mention my own, personal favorite solution to the luggage problem, which is currently only available on a few BMW motorcycles, but which has such great potential that I hope we soon see it on other makes and models: hard, locking, waterproof, and removable bags that are also expandable. I recently used these on tours of both Europe and South America and fell madly in love with them. Like nearly all BMW

Though the sign says the speed limit is 50 kilometers per hour, on many of Europe's crowded mountain roads that figure can be wildly optimistic. You may be lucky to see the far side of 40 kilometers per hour for more than a few seconds at a time. Under such circumstances, a 300-kilometer-per-hour sportbike makes little sense.

accessories, they're outrageously expensive and not too terribly attractive, but they're also incredibly functional. Constructed of lightweight and durable aluminum, they can be compressed to a very narrow profile against the bike, keeping the weight centered and low; with a snap of a couple of interior latches, they can be expanded to full touring size when needed. With these I could have very slim, unobtrusive bags when I was wearing my heavyweight, cold-weather gear, and when I needed to pack it away, I still had the carrying space I needed. It's a unique and very versatile system.

5. How Much Carrying Capacity Does It Have?

Though it may not seem so, this is an entirely different question than how much luggage capacity the bike has. For years one of my pet peeves has been that many bikes sold as "touring" machines are modifications of models that weren't originally designed for touring duty, and therefore simply don't have the kind of frame and suspensions needed to handle the extra weight. The best examples of this are some of the cruiser touring bikes that have had fairings or windshields added to them, along with saddlebags and/or trunks, to convert them to "touring models." In many cases, you'll find that a bike like this has already maxed out its carrying capacity by the time you throw a leg over it, without packing even an ounce of luggage into the bags, let alone adding a passenger to the rear seat.

Figuring this out for yourself will take a little effort, but it's well worth your time. First, you need to find out the "wet weight" of the bike. You can take the easy route and find a magazine that actually lists the bike's wet weight, or sometimes you'll find this number in the bike's specifications, but more often you won't. Manufacturers like to list the "dry weight" of their machines, which is the bike without any gasoline or oil in it; in some cases they don't even add the battery when calculating the real or "wet" weight! (In most cases, a full tank of gas and a full crankcase of oil will add approximately 42 pounds to the weight of a touring bike.) Accessories and options aren't added into the bike's weight, so you'll need to find out or approximate what those will weigh—you might be surprised to learn that standard pieces of equipment on a full-dress touring bike (the windshield, running lights, floorboards, luggage racks, backrests, radio equipment, heated seats or grips, alarm systems, GPS, and so on) can be considered accessories, and therefore aren't included when a factory calculates a bike's total dry weight.

Once you've added up all the items and fluids to get the wet weight, you'll need to subtract that weight from the bike's gross vehicle weight rating (GVWR) to find out exactly how much weight it can carry, including yourself, any luggage you want to bring, and/or a passenger.

On a very recent brand-new touring bike, I carefully researched the above items, did my calculations, and found that the bike, ready to roll, had a carrying capacity of 254 pounds. Considering that I weigh 265 pounds, the minute I threw a leg over the saddle, I was already overloading the bike beyond its legal carrying capacity by 11 pounds, and that was without my wife or any luggage whatsoever. If I wanted to tour on this bike, I was going to need about $2,000 in suspension upgrades. That's why you'll see dozens of vendors selling aftermarket suspension components at major motorcycle rallies, and usually doing a very brisk business. To my mind, the fact that bikes sold for touring are more often than not ill-equipped for the duty is one of the most shameful aspects of our sport.

> For many riders, the best possible scenario is found with the dedicated sport-touring machines like the Honda ST, Yamaha FJR, BMW RT, Kawasaki Concours, and others...

Parable:
Changing Tastes

Despite everything written above, the fact remains that it's likely no one bike is going to meet all your needs and wants throughout your riding life. The best we can hope for is either a series of reasonable compromises, or, if we're really lucky, eventually being able to add extra bikes to our stables. For the most fanatical among us, the ideal situation would be to someday reach the point where we owned a sport bike for canyon carving, a sport-tourer for weekend trips, a luxury tourer for taking Momma on vacation, a small commuter for work, a dual-sport or dirt bike for getting frisky now and then, and perhaps even a vintage machine for the occasional classic bike rally or Sunday ride down memory lane.

Most of us will never achieve that kind of status, but it's fun to dream. In the meantime, here's a little personal history of my own changing tastes through nearly 40 years of motorcycling.

I began riding in late 1971, about 39 years ago. My first three bikes were all what we would call "dual-sports" today, though I don't recall ever hearing that term back then. Most people called them "combination bikes," simply meaning they could be ridden both on and off-road. They had high fenders and pipes, engine bash plates, and knobby tires, but they were also equipped with regulation headlights, turn signals, and other equipment to make them completely street legal.

I rode these bikes back and forth to work every day, then on dirt trails in the Rocky Mountains (I lived in Colorado at the time) on the weekends. Every now and then I would enter an amateur motocross or enduro, and once I even participated in an ice-racing event held on the frozen Longmont Reservoir in January. I believe my bike at the time was a 1973 Yamaha 250 Enduro, but I could be

BMW's single-cylinder 650cc machine may not be my first choice for a cross-country jaunt in the United States, but when riding solo through any mountainous region, it's at the very top of my list.

wrong about that—it's been a long time. My wife and I took some short, weekend tours on our bikes, even the ones that didn't have a rear seat or passenger footpegs, believe it or not. I remember a two-day, 500-mile ride through the mountains where she rode on the back of our Kawasaki K100, sitting on a folded beach towel bungied down to the back fender! (I should note that back then she weighed a whopping 87 pounds, dripping wet.)

Around 1975 I bought my first pure streetbike, a Honda 400 Supersport. This style was called a "cafe racer." It had low, narrow handlebars (pseudo clip-ons), a four-into-one performance exhaust, and a six-speed gearbox, almost unheard of at the time. After fitting the 400 with a racing can and K&N air filters, I actually did a little bit of amateur racing with it, though I was never very competitive. Like all my other bikes, the Supersport's primary function was as my day-to-day commuter.

My wife and I were both really beginning to enjoy our weekend bike trips by then, so we started looking for a bike better suited for touring. We first set our sights on getting a BMW, since everyone said the big boxers were the ultimate for touring, but quickly found we couldn't even afford a well-used Beemer. A close friend had just purchased one of the first-ever Honda Gold Wings, and we fell in love with it, but again, the price was well out of range our budget, and there weren't any used ones available since the model was only a year old at the time. We eventually settled for a used Honda CX500, which we fitted with a Vetter Windjammer fairing and a set of Califia saddlebags. We didn't realize it at the time, but we had basically created our own version of what Honda would later market as the Silver Wing.

After that we owned a couple of CB750s, some KZs, and a few other bikes, including a CB200T that took over commuting duties to reduce the amount of wear and tear on my weekend and touring bikes. That was until 1981, when we finally bought our first (used) Gold Wing. From then on, we stuck exclusively with Wings for the next 10 years, owning a succession of GL1100s, GL1200s, and eventually a GL1500SE.

By that time I was working for the Gold Wing Road Riders Association (GWRRA), so naturally no other bike was even up for consideration. But in late 1990, I went to work for Bob Carpenter at **Road Rider** magazine, and a whole new vista of motorcycling opened up for me. Bob told me right off that my motorcycling education needed to be broadened, so he sent me out on a series of press intros and test rides with the various manufacturers. Since then, as near as I can figure, I've ridden about 350 different motorcycles. And you know what? I learned to appreciate the differences and to enjoy virtually every one of them on their own merits. Some were only weekend rides or a day on the test track, but I've ridden coast-to-coast and back again on Honda GLs, a Shadow 1100, ST1100, and 750 Nighthawk; on a Harley-Davidson Electra Glide and Road King; on a BMW R1100RT and F650CS; on a Kawasaki Concours and Voyager 1200; and on a Suzuki Katana and Yamaha Venture. I've also toured at least six foreign countries on a succession of other bikes.

Thinking back on all those long rides, I can honestly say that I enjoyed each and every one of them. However, I should add one small caveat: don't take my words to mean that I've loved absolutely every single motorcycle I've ever ridden. They're only true for 99.9 percent of them, and every "production" bike except one. The lone exception for a mass-produced bike would be the early Gilroy version of the Indian Scout, and the others would be a couple of one-off "designer" customs. The only redeeming virtue I could ever find in one of those was in styling, and style has just never been a major priority for me. I'll admit, of course, that it might be of paramount importance to some people, but I'm afraid that I am so narrow-minded that I simply cannot think of those people as "motorcyclists," but rather as "motorcycle owners."

Along the way, my own taste in bikes has changed somewhat. There was a time when I wouldn't own a bike with a windshield, for example, and now I'm not really interested in one without. There was also a period when I became so enamored of electronic goodies like intercoms and stereos that I hated to ride without them. Now it really doesn't matter to me anymore. Over the years, my major motorcycle priorities have slowly evolved from economy, to performance, to comfort, and are now starting to edge back toward performance once again. I'll still opt for a GL if the wife and I are going on a long tour, but if I'm distance-touring alone, I prefer a sport-tourer like an ST or RT. And if I'm only going on a relatively short tour, or one that doesn't involve much mountain twisty riding, I really prefer a cruiser tourer like the Yamaha Royal Star Tour Deluxe, or even a Harley Road King. But if I have a weekend of canyon carving with my buddies, give me a Suzuki SV650, or if I'm touring in a country like Brazil, with a lot of narrow roads and cobblestone streets, give me a BMW F650 or a Kawasaki KLR.

Obviously I am exceptionally fortunate; I've had the opportunity to ride almost anything and everything

Honda may have just introduced the perfect solo touring bike with the NT700V (that is, if you can afford the steep $10,000 sticker price).

manufacturers can dream up. Maybe that's why I find the nit-picking snobbery among aficionados of a particular brand, marque, or even type of motorcycle, so ludicrous, especially when it comes from riders who've never experienced any type of bike other than the one they own. While I've been guilty of this kind of snobbery at times, at least I can say that the very few bikes I've disliked only gained my disapproval after I actually studied them up close and rode them.

So I guess what I'm saying is, until you've ridden a mile (or a few hundred, really) in another guy's boots, you shouldn't judge him or his bike. As they say, "There's a bike for every butt."

When Honda introduced the GL1000 Gold Wing, the motorcycle press didn't quite know what to make of it. The public did: a full-dress touring bike.

After half a decade of watching customers spending hundreds and even thousands of dollars purchasing touring equipment for their Gold Wings, Honda wised up and brought out the Interstate, a motorcycle that came equipped with full touring gear.

Honda proved everyone wrong when the firm's new GL1000 Gold Wing made its debut at the Intermot Motorcycle Show in October 1974. Instead of going head-to-head against Kawasaki and producing the world's fastest motorcycle, Honda had a different target for the new Gold Wing: BMW. From its sedate bodywork to its boxer-type opposed-cylinder engine configuration to its shaft final drive, Honda's new heavyweight followed a formula laid out by BMW designer Max Friz more than five decades earlier. Honda simply took the virtues of BMW's genteel motorcycles and added more of everything: more cylinders (four for the Wing versus two for the

Beemer), more technology (liquid-cooling versus air-cooling, overhead cams versus pushrods), more displacement (999cc versus 898cc for the biggest BMW models), and more weight—the new Honda topped 600 pounds fully fueled, 100 pounds more than a comparable BMW and heavier than any mass-produced motorcycle made except for the biggest Harley-Davidson models.

At first the motorcycle buying public didn't know quite know what to make of Honda's new ultimate behemoth. They thought of it as a sort of 't'ain't—it ain't a performance bike and it ain't a custom-styled bike—and Honda only sold 13,000 units in the U.S. market for the 1975 model year,

Honda upgraded both the touring amenities and the handling and performance of the Gold Wing when it brought out the 1200cc version of its ultimate touring bike.

Keep in mind that the category of touring motorcycle hadn't really been invented yet, especially in the key U.S. market. At that time, no mass-produced motorcycle came with a fairing as standard equipment, with the exception of a few European sportbikes that were imported into the U.S. market in such miniscule numbers that virtually no one had even seen one, except perhaps in the pages of a magazine. The closest thing to a factory touring bike was a Harley-Davidson Electra Glide fitted with the optional Tour Pak, which consisted of a handlebar-mounted batwing fairing, fiberglass saddlebags, and a fiberglass trunk.

But this status quo was rapidly changing, thanks to the Vetter Fairing Company (see the sidebar in chapter one), which was coming on like gangbusters at just about the same time that the Gold Wing hit the market. Honda's Gold Wing and Vetter's Windjammer Fairing intersected at a fortuitous nexus, giving birth to an entirely new

genre of motorcycle: the full-dress touring bike. Riders soon realized that the Wing was the perfect platform for Vetter's fairings and saddlebags, and soon virtually every Gold Wing sold sported Vetter bodywork. By the time the GL1000 was replaced by the GL1100 for the 1980 model year, Honda had sold nearly 100,000 Gold Wings in the U.S. market alone.

BMW hadn't taken Honda's intrusion on its traditional turf lightly, and for 1979 BMW had one upped the Japanese manufacturer by introducing R100RT, a motorcycle that came from the factory outfitted with complete touring bodywork. Honda responded by offering the Interstate, a version of the new GL1100 Gold Wing that came outfitted with complete touring bodywork. Soon every manufacturer offered a fully-dressed touring bike in its model lineup (a situation that contributed to the eventual bankruptcy of the Vetter Fairing Company). To keep ahead of the crowd, Honda offered an Aspencade version of its Gold Wing Interstate, a bike that came equipped with every luxury item available, like a stereo with CB radio and an onboard air compressor for adjusting the bike's air suspension system. When the competition would step up their game and introduce a bike to challenge the Gold Wing's supremacy in the touring bike market, Honda would fight back, adding more features and, for the 1984 model year, more displacement.

Finally Honda exercised the nuclear option. Honda had toyed with the idea of a six-cylinder version of the Gold Wing since the very beginning of the model's development, when early test mules featured six-cylinder engines instead of four-cylinder examples. The concept had proved promising, but Honda had elected to go the conservative route and chosen a more conventional four-cylinder configuration for production. But Honda, a traditional proponent of six-cylinder engines, continued developing the design, and

when it came time to upgrade the GL1200 Gold Wing for the 1988 model year, the company introduced the GL1500 version that featured a 1,520cc opposed six-cylinder engine in place of the four-cylinder design of previous models.

The bike was heavy, weighing well over 800 pounds when filled with fluids, but it carried its weight well, thanks to the centralized mass of the opposed-cylinder engine and the corresponding low center of gravity. If it weighed too much for a rider to handle, the bike featured a handy reverse gear that relied on the starter motor to spin the rear wheel backwards. All in all, the GL1500 Gold Wing was so close to perfect that all the other manufacturers simply abandoned the touring market rather than trying to compete with the almighty Honda.

The GL1500 Gold Wing proved so good that the model soldiered on with only minor changes for 13 years. Eventually Honda had some competition in the touring market, in the form

The GL1500 wasn't the first six-cylinder motorcycle Honda had produced. The company had fielded six-cylinder grand prix racing bikes back in the 1960s. It wasn't even the first six-cylinder streetbike the company had produced; that honor went to the CBX, introduced in the late 1970s. The six-cylinder Gold Wing was, however, the finest touring motorcycle on the planet. It was so good that it was produced virtually unchanged for 13 years.

the BMW K1200LT, introduced for the 1999 model year. With more power, more creature comforts, and less weight than the Wing, the biggest Beemer presented a formidable competitor. Honda responded by speeding up development of the next-generation Gold Wing and introduced the GL1800 for the 2001 model year. Though its new fuel-injected six-cylinder engine now displaced the 1,832cc, the GL1800 Gold Wing weighed less than the GL1500 version, thanks in large part to a new aluminum frame.

Once again Honda had brought a gun to a knife fight, forcing all the other players to tuck their tails tightly between their legs and slink off

the field of battle. Harley-Davidson, of course, continues to sell its venerable Electra Glide, but with its pushrod air-cooled twin-cylinder engine and handlebar-mounted fairing, it cannot be considered in the same class as the Gold Wing. BMW continues to produce the K1200LT virtually unchanged, but sales decrease every year; the only reason the model remains in the lineup is because BMW has long ago amortized the tooling costs and what few K1200LT models it continues to sell, it sells at a tremendous profit margin. Otherwise the world's motorcycle manufacturers have once again ceded the heavyweight luxury touring market to King Gold Wing.

The six-cylinder Gold Wing was something of a shocker to the motorcycling public, but it was an evolution of the GL platform that had been envisioned within Honda since the very beginning. In fact, early development mules like this one featured six-cylinder engines early on in the development of the original GL1000.

In the early 2000s the original six-cylinder GL1500 was finally starting to show its age, so Honda introduced the GL1800. With its aluminum frame and fuel-injected engine, the GL1800 was as dramatic an improvement over its predecessor as the GL1500 had been over four-cylinder versions.

With the GL1800 Honda once again leapfrogged over its competition. It was so good that every other manufacturer virtually abandoned the heavyweight luxury-touring market. Will this version last as long as did its predecessor? Most likely—when you combine a weak economy that's dampening motorcycle sales and no serious competition from any other manufacturer with the fact that the current Wing has no major flaws, you'll see that there's very little reason to fix what ain't broken.

Chapter 3

Avoiding Common Pitfalls When Choosing a Bike

Resist Buying the Latest and Greatest

Unfortunately, our love of motorcycles is often used against us by the manufacturers' clever marketing agents. When a new model, or a totally new version of an existing model is about to come out, millions of dollars are spent to generate media hype that will hopefully trigger a feeding frenzy in local dealership showrooms. Believe me, after over 30 years in the motorcycle magazine business, I've seen it succeed time and time again. The bad part is that while sometimes the new bike lives up to the anticipation,

When your bike breaks down on tour, even in the middle of the Mojave Desert like this, knowing that parts are available in the next town really helps—even if one of your buddies has to ride 150 miles to get them!

more often than not it doesn't, and a whole lot of motorcyclists are left with a bad case of buyer's remorse. I could easily name at least four bikes from the past 20 years that were heralded with great fanfare on TV and in the magazines, and were each named "Bike of the Year" by at least two different, national motorcycling magazines, only to be completely dropped from the manufacturer's lineup within the next 18 months. Even those bikes that are carefully designed and destined to become great successes usually go through a teething period during the first year or two of production. That means that the riders who jumped on the bandwagon early usually find themselves a year or two down the road owning a bike they paid too much for and that doesn't have the upgrades and fixes that were applied later.

After many years, hundreds of bikes, and over one million miles of touring, my personal favorite bikes come down to a handful. For sport-touring, it is a virtual tossup between the Honda ST1300, the Yamaha FJR1300, and the BMW R1200RT (although I just recently toured on a new BMW K1300GT, and it may be my new personal favorite). I haven't ridden Honda's new VFR1200F (pictured) yet, but that looks like it might be in the running.

It's an all too common story, and yet, quite honestly, one that not only *will* repeat itself, but actually *must* repeat itself if any bike is to eventually reach its ultimate level of refinement. If no one bought the first models, there wouldn't be a second- or third-generation "improved" model for the rest of us. So let the other testosterone-pumped fanatics who don't read this book do your beta-testing for you. Be patient. Sit back. You won't die if you don't get the very first new bike on the block. Wait a year—or even better, two—then go out and buy the next generation, with the improved suspension, better brakes, or with that nagging overheating problem cured. You'll thank me for it in the long run.

Make Sure It Has Enough Range

Fortunately, lack of fuel capacity isn't nearly as big a problem as it was a few years back, but it's still important to check out the fuel capacity and approximate gas mileage of any bike you intend to use for touring. If you're a rider who's new to touring, even though you may have ridden for several years, fuel range is an item that can easily be overlooked. This can become

This Honda NT700 was just released as this book was being finished. You might think it would qualify for my warning about buying a new model, but actually it does not. You see, this model has actually been built and sold as the "Deauville" for many years in the European market. Do a little homework before accepting or rejecting any particular model.

painfully apparent if you're from a heavily populated area. For example: I once arranged a tour for a group of New England riders. We had their personal bikes transported to California to spend a week touring parts of the original Route 66, through Arizona, Nevada, and Southern California. Unfortunately, it didn't occur to me until the day we were unloading the bikes to leave that the two Harley 1200cc Sportsters that riders had brought, both of which were to be ridden two-up, each had an effective touring range of about 125 miles. And since there were at least two sections of our route where there were no gas stations for over 150 miles, we ended up having to carry a spare gas can in our utility trailer to top off the Sportsters on the road, out in the middle of the Mojave Desert. If you live and ride in an area where the gas stations are never more than 50 miles apart, like New England, it may not occur to you you may very well encounter a situation like this when touring.

Note the small, stylized fuel tank on this cruiser. Sure, it looks good, and the bike seems to have been modified for touring duty with the addition of a windshield and saddlebags, but what do you think the cruising range might be?

To my mind, any bike intended for use as a touring machine should be able to travel a minimum of 175 miles on a tank of gas, with a reserve capacity to carry you at least another 40 miles beyond that if necessary. And remember,

Continued on page 67

Parable:
Bigger and Better?

For myself, and probably also for most guys my age, I think the problem started in our formative years of grade school and high school. We grew up in what would later be termed the "muscle car" era, when it was unquestioned that as far as anything with a motor was concerned, bigger was always better.

I made pretty good money for a teenager, and my senior year in high school I managed to buy a

Chevy Impala convertible. I had it fitted out with sidewalls raised white letters (almost mandatory in those days for a car to be "cool"), glass-pac mufflers and styled mag wheels, but unfortunately, it **only** had a 283 cubic-inch V-8, which meant I couldn't quite run with the in crowd on Saturday nights. That particular group ran impromptu—and very illegal—drag races, just outside of town, at the end of what we called "the Belt." The group followed an unwritten law that dictated everyone

Honda's new VFR1200F is lighter and sportier than the admittedly heavy ST1300, but at the same time it offers ergonomics and passenger accommodations that are at least equal to the larger bike. Although classified as a sportbike, it might just be the best of both worlds.

with anything less than a 350 mill under his hood parked with the spectators. Never mind that I had my 283 fitted out with a Holley four-barrel and trick manifolds; the mantra was, "there's no replacement for displacement." Even the guys with hopped-up 350s were at the bottom of the food chain in those days, lorded over by those lucky enough to have a Chevy SS396, a Ford 390, or the rulers of the decade, the mighty MOPAR 426s and 440s in the various Dodge and Plymouth muscle cars.

A lot of us grew up to eventually become today's motorcyclists, but we never quite shook off the labels that were stamped on us back then. Though we might not be willing to admit it in public, we

still believe, deep in our hearts, that there's no replacement for displacement.

My favorite example of that prejudice goes back to 1999, when I was involved with the testing of two Triumph motorcycles: the Trophy 900 and the Trophy 1200. Though the 900 was a triple and the 1200 a four-cylinder, in virtually all other respects the two bikes were mechanically identical. In fact, they shared the same engine block, but the 1200 had another cylinder grafted on. Otherwise, the frame, suspension, transmission, bodywork, and even the engine's bore and stroke and compression ratio, were all the same. In performance testing, the 1200 Trophy (actually 1180ccs) developed 106

For the long haul, two-up, there is no doubt in my mind that the Wing is still king. I think some of the touring cruisers like this Kawasaki might actually top it in comfort, but the power and handling just aren't quite there.

For the twisties of the Alps, Dolomites, or almost anywhere in Europe, give me a BMW F650GS, a Kawasaki KLR650, or my new personal favorite: a Suzuki V-Strom 650.

The 680cc V-twin in Honda's NT700V might be a bit taxed hauling two plus-sized people and all their gear through the mountains, but it might be adequate for a couple of svelte folks who travel light.

horsepower, while the 900 Trophy (actually 885ccs) put out 98 horse power. The price of that extra 8 horse power was having 34 pounds of weight added to the bike and having your wallet lightened by a little over $1,000. And though you gained eight whole horses with the big Trophy, in real-world testing the smaller triple actually got through the quarter-mile quicker, stopped shorter, cornered better, and was generally ranked by everyone who rode the two as the better-handling machine. Tests in the various motorcycle magazines around the world seemed to support all of these conclusions, but can you guess which model outsold the other by about two to one here in the U.S.? The 1200, the one with the bigger numbers on the spec sheet but lower horsepower-to-weight ratio. Pretty much the same scenario was played out a year or two later by Honda's VTX1800 versus the VTX1300.

A few years back, I got the opportunity to do an off-road ride through Death Valley, aboard a BMW R1200GS. Quite frankly, it was a grueling experience. Though the big GS is undoubtedly a superlative machine, in the deep, soft sand of Death Valley, it was more than I could handle. By the end of each day, I had dropped the bike several times and was totally exhausted from muscling its bulk as it wallowed around axle-deep in the sand. But as luck would have it, I got the chance to ride almost all of the same routes about a year later aboard the Suzuki V-Strom 650, and though I had to switch to some tires that were knobbier than the stock units for the trip, I found the experience totally satisfying. Even though the big GS obviously had more horsepower and about three-quarters of an inch more ground clearance, the nearly 80-pound less weight carried by the Suzuki made all the difference in the world. I never dropped the

'Strom, probably because it just didn't sink so deep in the sand, and I didn't have to work half as hard to control my line.

That experience, and some good advice from other riders, played a part in my decision the next year to acquire a BMW F650GS for my 20-day ride through the Alps. I must admit, I was a bit apprehensive that the "little" bike would be out of its league on the legendary mountain roads, but I was not disappointed in the least. For those who haven't yet had the pleasure, I can tell you that many of the Alpine passes are so narrow, steep, and twisty, that you can ride all day without ever getting above third gear and averaging no more than 40 miles per hour all day. I can't tell you how many big sportbikes I passed during that trip, but

it was a lot. Their big engines were nothing more than extra weight to carry around, and I could see how hard the riders were working to make the constant transitions from full-lean-left to full-lean-right, while the little GS was dancing underneath me with no more than fingertip inputs.

Nowadays, with the advances in engine and frame technology, metallurgy, tire design, aerodynamics, and the many other disciplines that contribute to motorcycle design, it seems we have reached a point of diminishing returns when it comes to sheer size. I know that on some racetracks these days, it's not at all uncommon to see 600cc race bikes posting faster lap times than the liter-plus classes. Certainly a bigger engine gives you the advantage in a straight line, but its sheer bulk

Bigger isn't necessarily always better. Don't count out the new touring scooters, like this Suzuki Burgman. This couple toured several thousand miles with a group of Gold Wings and never had trouble keeping up. In terms of comfort, carrying capacity, and range, the Burgman deserves the touring moniker.

Kawasaki's venerable KLR650 may be thought of primarily as a dual-sport machine, but it serves admirably on the pavement and makes a great long-range touring mount.

In addition to the obvious advantages of lower weight, easier handling, and better gas mileage, the new crop of middleweight dual-sport bikes allow you the opportunity to stray from the pavement now and then and explore areas a pure touring machine will never see. Perhaps this is why dual-sporting is the fastest-growing segment within motorcycling.

also makes a bike harder to accelerate, slower to brake, and more difficult to transition into and out of turns.

That's not to say that, depending on the situation, a larger bike isn't the answer. For example, when I run my guided tours, I ride a Honda GL1800. For the type of roads I ride, the load I need to carry, and the comfort I want for long days in the saddle, there's no doubt the Wing is king. But if I'm riding the same route alone and get the chance, I'll switch to an ST1300 or FJR in a heartbeat. And if I know I'm going to get the opportunity to stray off onto the unpaved "shortcuts" across the desert, then I'll try to get my hands on a V-Strom 650, a small GS, or perhaps even a KLR. It's simply a matter of choosing the right tool for the job at hand.

Thinking that bigger is better is a mistake. I'm sure you've seen it just as much as I have: those new riders out there buying way too much bike for the job, or for their skill level, because of the unintentional peer pressure we've put on them to buy the new 2000 or 2300cc monster that isn't going to do anything for them except expand their egos.

I am certainly not saying that a smaller bike is always going to be the better choice, but we need to wean ourselves away from our teenage belief that bigger is always better, because it's not.

Continued from page 61

when touring, especially two-up with a full complement of luggage, you're likely to get considerably less fuel mileage than you would when just going out solo for a day trip.

As much as I hate to single out any particular type of bike, the truth is that this problem is most prevalent with the same class I criticized for often not having sufficient load capacity—the cruiser tourers—and for the same reason again: they weren't originally designed for touring.

Parts and Service Availability Is Important!

Much like the problem with fuel range, the problem of universal parts and service availability is something that probably wouldn't occur to a new tourer.

If you're all alone, it doesn't much matter if the parts are at a BMW dealer 250 miles away or a Honda dealer only 100 miles away.

No matter what you ride, if you're never more than an hour or two away from a dealer (or your home, for that matter), then a breakdown is no more than a minor inconvenience. This is definitely not true when touring.

This issue is another good argument for not buying the latest and greatest new model of bike, as we discussed above, because even the manufacturer's dealerships probably won't stock much in the way of replacement parts for their newest models. I once had a guy on tour with me who'd just purchased a model that had only been released weeks before. The man suffered the indignity of having someone back into his bike in a parking lot and knock it over. The damage was minor—just a broken shift lever—and there was a dealership only a few miles away, but the shift levers for that model weren't in stock yet, and even a special order would've taken three to five days to arrive. He ended up having to rent a car to finish the trip.

Secondly, it's important that no matter what brand of bike you choose, you should check that it uses a relatively common size of battery and tires. These are the two items most likely to fail or become damaged on the road; if your bike was built to use an oddball tire size, or a battery that was specially

A really nice couple we enjoyed having on tour with us. Unfortunately that Harley only had a two-up touring range of about 100 miles, and there were places on the tour without gas for 150 miles and more. We had to have one of the tour guides carry extra fuel for them. To my mind, no touring bike should have an effective range shorter than 200 miles; I prefer at least 250.

designed to fit only that model, you're risking your entire trip. Before I learned this lesson the hard way, I once had to purchase a small car battery, put it in one of my saddlebags, and jury-rig cables to my bike's electrical system to get home.

Bigger Isn't Necessarily Better
Do me a favor and think seriously about that statement for a moment. Then read on.

The Renting Alternative

A few years ago, I spent a week taking a training class on how to run a motorcycle rental franchise. There was a lot more to learn than I originally thought, especially in terms of the insurance and legalities involved, but I managed to muddle through it and went back to Connecticut to help open up a new, full-service motorcycle rental agency for my employers. A year later, I would return to California and open my own motorcycle rental and touring agency.

Quite frankly, when I learned how expensive it was to rent bikes, I didn't think we'd get much traffic. But that didn't really matter much, because we were looking at having a rental agency mainly as a sales tool. For one thing, it gave us the flexibility to be able to offer demo rides on our rental bikes. We all know that one of the biggest problems with motorcycle dealerships is their inability, for insurance and liability reasons, to allow customers to try out bikes. In addition, once you let someone ride

> For some reason, people have no problem at all buying a "new" car with a couple hundred demo miles on it, but most motorcyclists won't touch a bike with the same mileage if they're looking to buy new.

a new bike, it's no longer new and has to be heavily discounted and sold as a used bike. For some reason, people have no problem at all buying a "new" car with a couple hundred demo miles on it, but most motorcyclists won't touch a bike with the same mileage if they're looking to buy new. We countered that problem with a fairly simple deal: If you were looking to buy a new Gold Wing, for example, and had never been on one, we would rent you a Wing for a couple of days. If you decided to buy a new Wing from us, we would take a weekend's

Continued on page 74

Parable:

It Ain't the Tool

Back when I was about 11 years old, I remember watching a pitchman at a carnival as he demonstrated a gyroscopic toy that he balanced on a string between his hands. He made the toy run back and forth on the string, turn upside down, do somersaults, and all kinds of other incredible stunts. I just had to have one, and shelled out my whole month's hard-earned allowance of $5 to get "one of the last ones left." Naturally, after getting back home with my prize, I found that I couldn't make it do any of the things the carney had demonstrated. It ended up in the back of my closet, an embarrassing reminder of how I'd been taken.

Legendary racer Walt Fulton, on the rear bike, passing me for about the 10,000th time. I know better than to try to keep up with him. Notice his body position compared to mine: shoulders and head low, elbows tucked in, and the balls of his feet on the pegs. Note that my feet are clear back on the heel. Most commonly, as in my case, the weakest part of the motorcycle is the person hanging onto the handlebars.

Months later, when confessing to my grandfather about what had happened, he pulled out an old pocketknife he always carried with him and held it up in front of me. "Remember when I carved you a toy airplane out of a block of wood with this knife?" he asked.

"Sure, Grandpa."

"Well, if I sold you this knife," he said, "do you think you could carve your own toy airplane with it?"

You wouldn't want to do a track day with a Honda Gold Wing, but it capable hands it can show its taillights to a sportbike that's piloted by a squid with more tattoos than riding skills.

"No, Grandpa. I don't know how."

"Exactly. It took me years to learn, and lots of practice. It ain't the tool, boy. It's the man operating it. Just like with your toy."

A couple of years later, that lesson stood me in good stead when a small-time con man came to a local playground and gathered a large crowd of preteens around himself by showing off with a yo-yo. I've never, before or since, seen anyone make a yo-yo do the things that guy could. Of course, after his demonstration, he opened up a suitcase full of brightly colored yo-yos and started selling them to all the kids for a buck apiece. Several kids ran home to break open their piggy banks just so they could get one. I was about the only holdout—standing there thinking about that gyro toy, and what my grandpa had said. Of course none of my friends could ever get their yo-yos to do any of the tricks they'd seen. Most of the toys broke after just a few hours of trying anyway, as they were very cheaply made. If that guy is still alive today, I'll bet he's on Channel 99 at 3 a.m., selling "kitchen magicians."

Fast-forward another 40 years. I'm riding up one of my favorite canyon roads, following my good friend Walt Fulton. We're just out for a little Sunday morning putt, but even when he's just dawdling along, Walt is a challenge for me to keep up with. Some of you older guys might recognize the name, but for those who don't, Walt is a former factory team racer for several different major motorcycle manufacturers, a four-time Daytona winner, and the guy who wore the helmet camera that filmed all those famous on-track racing scenes in the movie **On Any Sunday**. Even now, over 30 years later, Walt doesn't own a car, rides every day, and works as both a motorcycle riding instructor and a motorcycle accident reconstruction expert. I've never met, and probably never will meet, anyone with a greater understanding of the dynamics of motorcycling, or the skills to utilize that knowledge so effectively.

Anyway, there we were tooling up the mountain, when we came up behind two young men on what appeared to be very new and expensive hyper-bikes. One was definitely a Hayabusa, and I think the other was a CBR of some kind, though it'd been repainted and all the badging had been removed, so I couldn't be sure. Both bikes sported aftermarket exhausts, and from their sound probably had their

engines tricked out too. The riders both sported very expensive racing leathers in colors that matched their machines, complete with titanium kneepucks and those stylish new humps on the backs, to reduce air turbulence from the helmet when you're tucked in. All in all, they looked like very serious riders. However, the illusion was quickly dispelled as we went around a few curves together. Though their engines screamed a beautiful note as they revved up and downshifted, and each rider hung radically off his bike to touch a knee to the tarmac, their lines through the curves were wide and undisciplined, and their bikes' lean angles were actually fairly moderate. Everything about their appearance gave

BMW parallel twins may not look like sportbikes, but with their torque-laden engines and generous ground clearance, they can be formidable tools when the roads turn twisty.

the illusion of speed, except the actual speed wasn't there. Nor was the control, as they demonstrated by exiting each turn far too wide and well out of position to set up for the next corner.

It just so happened that on this particular day, rather than riding one of his newer, faster bikes, Walt was "exercising" a 15-year-old BMW Boxer of his that had, as I recall, about 100,000 miles under its wheels. The Boxer was bone stock, and by Walt's own admission was "overdue for a whole new suspension," because it was "handling pretty badly." Despite all that, after following the two superbikes through a couple more curves, when they swung wide through a long, right-hand sweeper, Walt simply downshifted the old Beemer and zipped past them both in a heartbeat—on the inside. He never changed his position on the seat or did anything trendy like sticking a knee out. He just leaned over, nailed the throttle, and smoothly and quickly knifed through the turn. I don't think either of the guys he passed even hit the apex of their turns before Walt was out the other end, straightening up and accelerating away.

Being a less accomplished rider, I waited for a longer, straighter opportunity to pass, and caught up with Walt at a pre-determined coffee shop a few miles away. As we sat there warming up and relaxing, the two pseudo-streetfighters buzzed past and Walt said, "I was hoping they might stop in here. I would really like to try to talk them into getting some decent training. It's not just that they'd enjoy riding so much more, but if they keep up like that, somebody is going to get seriously hurt." I nodded in agreement as he continued. "It's a shame that so many of these young riders nowadays think it's all about buying the best or fastest or most expensive bike they can find. Or maybe even worse, that they think that if they buy the trickest Yoshimura exhaust can, or trendiest race tire or Ohlins suspension or whatever, that it will make them ride better. Sure, those things will give you an edge, but only if you've already mastered the basics—and they don't have a clue about the basics."

Kawasaki's KLR650 isn't exactly a speed demon in a straight line, but on extremely tight roads few bikes can keep up with it.

At that moment, for the first time in over 40 years, I saw my grandfather's face again, and heard those words: "It ain't the tool, boy—it's the man operating it."

Continued from page 69

rental fees off the purchase price. Even better, if you bought the very same bike you rented, we would deduct up to a week of rental fees off the purchase price.

Well, that was the mindset we started out with, but to our surprise, we began renting out the majority of our fleet almost immediately and with virtually no advertising at all. By spring we'd tripled the size of our fleet and were advertising fairly extensively. The way things looked, the rental agency could become a fairly good little profit-maker all on its own. Any extra retail sales it generated were pure gravy. And that, my friends, seems to be the case all over the country to this day.

Six months after starting up our agency, I attended a convention of motorcycle rental agency owners and operators. After three days of talking with dozens of them, I realized they were almost all expanding their businesses, and had very good feelings about the future of the rental business; now I know why.

BMW's K1200LT was so good that it forced Honda to speed up development of the GL1800. This is the last BMW to feature the old laid-down "Flying Brick" four-cylinder engine.

The largest motorcycle rental company in the world is EagleRider Motorcycle Rentals, headquartered in Los Angeles. They have 32 rental locations in the U.S., plus one each in Spain, France, and Mexico. A lot of people who've heard about EagleRider think they're a Harley-only rental agency, and though that was true several years ago, it's no longer the case. They now rent Hondas, BMWs, and several other brands, depending on the location, and also rent ATVs, watercraft, and snowmobiles. In 2003 they rented to about 18,000 customers. Just three years later, by the end of 2006, they had rented to over 38,000 customers, and current projections have them renting to 60,000 customers before the end of next year.

I tell you all this just to make you understand that it isn't just my opinion that motorcycle rentals are growing in popularity. The market is, in truth, practically exploding. The only question then is why?

Well first of all, there is the fact that a lot of people who wouldn't necessarily be interested in owning a bike full-time are still very

Then too, there is the convenience of being able to fly to some far-off destination and rent a bike for a few days, thus conserving valuable vacation time.

interested in going for a weekend ride now and then, or perhaps even taking a motorcycling vacation. Then too, there is the convenience of being able to fly to some far-off destination and rent a bike for a few days, thus conserving valuable vacation time. If you live in Maine and want to attend Sturgis, or you live in California and want to see Americade in New York, you need at least three weeks to ride or trailer your bike back and forth, attend the event, and get back home. But in just one week you could fly out, grab your rental bike, have fun at the rally for five or six days, drop off the bike, and fly home. No muss, no fuss.

As I told you at the beginning, I was a bit taken aback by the prices for rentals. For a full-size touring bike like a Honda GL or Harley Electra Glide, the rental price is around $130 per day. Add in the taxes, insurance, and things like "environmental recovery fees," and you're going to be out about $165 per day. Of course there are discounts for multiple-day rentals, but still, a week's rental will usually run you close to $1200. Our most popular rental at our agency is the Three-Day Special, which runs about $450. Okay, that sounds like a lot, but think about this: in New England, only about 20 weekends fall within what would be considered the riding season. During one recent year, the weather was miserable for nine of those weekends. That left 11 "rideable" weekends. And unless you were a die-hard enthusiast, you probably would have ridden on only about half of those opportunities, or maybe six weekends out of the entire year. If you bought a new Wing or Glide and financed it, your payments would be about $4,000 per year, your insurance about $500, taxes and license about $300, and your maintenance costs about $250. That's $5,050 per year to ride, probably for five years, after which you would own a five-year-old bike. If you rented a

If you go the touring cruiser route, make certain that the bike you select has adequate fuel range and adequate carrying capacity.

bike from Friday through Monday for the six weekends you rode, you would spend $2,700 per year to ride. Even if you rode every one of the nice weekends (all 11) in the year, and rented a bike from Friday night until Sunday night, your total cost would be about $3,630 at the end of the year, or $1420 less per year than owning the same bike. And you wouldn't have to buy tires, change the oil, or even wash and wax the darned thing. Not to mention, each week you'd have a new bike, fully serviced and checked out, polished, and ready to ride. You could even get a different color, or even a different model, each week. Sure, at the end of five years you wouldn't own a five-year-old bike. But you'd also be over $7,000 ahead in expenditures.

I was beginning to understand.

For maximum luggage capacity, you can't beat a Gold Wing, especially one like this—fitted with a luggage rack and extra bag on top of the trunk. If the two of you can't carry what your touring needs on a Wing, you should probably look into Amtrak.

Chapter 4

Planning a Tour

Where to Go and How to Get There

One could easily write an entire book on just this subject. If I started getting into the specifics of great places to travel on a bike, I probably wouldn't be able to finish in my lifetime. Heck, I think I could write over 1,000 pages just on the reasons you should take a motorcycle tour through New Zealand, my own personal favorite place to ride.

In addition to being a good way to start your touring career, a group tour is also a great way to make friends. One of the things I've always enjoyed most is organizing tours to share some of my favorite places with new people. When I moved to Connecticut for a couple of years, I decided I really wanted to show my New England friends my old stomping grounds in the Southwest, so I organized this tour group to take them all to Death Valley.

For starters, though, let us consider that there are two basics types of motorcycle tours: destination-oriented and travel-oriented. Of course, in reality, all tours or rides of any kind are in some way destination-oriented, as there's always a place you intend to end up, but it's also true that for touring riders, even when we're riding to reach a specific location at a specific time, we'll do everything in our power to sublimate the destination to the actual tour. In other words, to follow the old touring riders' mantra, "it ain't the destination, it's the journey."

My touring mentor Bob Carpenter, the longtime editor of *Road Rider* magazine, used to say that the best kind of motorcycle ride was a "circle tour," meaning that when you left home, you had no specific route, itinerary, timeline, or destination in mind at the outset other than to eventually arrive back where you started. This, I think, may be the very essence of the perfect motorcycle tour.

So, rather than give you some kind of list of places to go on your bike, I would prefer to try to help you learn how to create your own list, or to put it more simply, how to . . .

Rate the Ride

Considering the different jobs I've held over the past 40 years, I've had the unique good fortune to tour on a variety of motorcycles through more venues than probably 90 percent of the touring riders in the world. That being the case, I'm often asked the question, "Where's the best place to ride?"

Obviously this is a much more difficult question to answer than it would seem on the surface. For starters, how any individual rider would rate any particular ride is going to be determined to a large degree by that rider's particular preferences in terms of riding style. Do you prefer really tight, technically challenging roads, or are wide, high-speed sweepers more your style? Is beautiful scenery important to you? Density of traffic? Neat things to see and do along the way? Are high speed limits, or even the lack of speed limits a high priority? Do you ride a full-dress touring bike, a sport-tourer, a cruiser, a dual-sport, or a sport bike? The best rides for one may very well be a pain in the ass for others.

So, when I started thinking about coming up with some kind of rating system for different touring venues, about all I could do was base my criteria on my personal preferences. With that in mind, I eventually came up with a point system of sorts, based on a simple 10-point score for each category, with 10 being a virtually unattainable perfect score.

Okay, so those are my 10 personal criteria for rating a touring ride. With each category at least technically capable of earning 10 points, the total for any ride

These are the categories I determined:

Ride Quality

Number and length of sections within the tour that are at least moderately challenging to my riding skills. Points deducted for long, straight, and boring sections, or time spent passing through densely populated areas.

Road Quality

Smooth, well-maintained, and even surfaces with a good traction coefficient rate highest. Points deducted for frequency of potholes, sand, or gravel.

Traffic

Based not just on the frequency of other vehicles encountered, but also the type, and the courtesy of the local drivers.

Expense

The less a tour costs me, the longer and farther I can ride. From country to country, or even between different areas within one country, there can be huge discrepancies in the costs of fuel, food, and lodging.

Variety

A couple of days of the same kind of riding is fine, but I don't want to do the same thing over and over for six or seven days straight. A mix of different roads and terrain is more appealing to me.

Weather Conditions

Certainly I have no control over the weather, but by the same token I wouldn't choose to ride in Canada in December any more than to ride in the Mojave Desert in August. I want to ride in a climate that's fairly temperate at the time I'll be there.

Exotic Appeal

This can be anything from riding where they speak a different language than I do to riding on the "other" side of the road. I enjoy mingling with other cultures, trying strange foods, and even being challenged by something as simple as finding different electrical outlets in the wall sockets or trying to figure out how that toilet flushes.

Scenery

I think most touring riders are like me, in that we really enjoy expansive scenery. Percentage-wise, you see a lot more bikes pulled off at scenic lookouts than you do cars.

Off-Bike Attractions

When the riding day is done, the touring isn't over. It's great to end the day's riding at a location where there's something interesting to see or do.

Bragging Rights

This is the toughest one to own up to, but if we're honest with ourselves, I think we all know that our decision to ride many times is at least partly based on desire to say, "been there, done that!"

could conceivably total 100 points—though in reality, we all know that a "perfect" ride doesn't exist . . . at least not in this world. I have to admit that my wife helped with deciding on the criteria, and is allowed input in deciding the ratings after our rides, since she tours along with me most of the time and her satisfaction with the ride definitely influences my own.

So, just where's the best place to ride? Here are my top five ratings, with a tie for fifth place:

91 points –   South Island, New Zealand
89 points –   Swiss/Austrian Alps
85 points –   Dolomites of northeast Italy
81 points –   Adirondacks of northeast New York
79 points –   Blue Ridge Parkway of North Carolina
79 points –   Utah Canyonlands

An adventure-tourer, like our friend in the photo, will have an entirely different set of criteria for planning a route than, say, someone more into luxury touring. Only you can determine what suits your bike and riding style, though I encourage you to experiment with routes you wouldn't normally take. You never know— you might discover a whole new set of interests. We tour because we like things that are out of the mainstream, don't we?

Any one of you could probably use the same set of criteria and come up with an entirely different list. It's also worth noting that I can only rate those places I've personally experienced, and base my rating on the short time that I experienced them. As an example of how fickle and totally unscientific this system can be, I've ridden through the Utah Canyonlands area at least six times, and if I based my rating on only the first trip, the area would probably have rated much lower because I encountered particularly bad weather, bad traffic, and road construction during that ride. But subsequent journeys were much more pleasant, bringing the total rating experience to a considerably higher level.

Of course, if you're planning a tour, or just thinking of places you might like to ride and haven't visited yet, pre-rating a ride is going to be a challenge. Still, it can be done, at least to a certain degree, by talking to others who have made the ride, or reading their accounts in motorcycling magazines and newsletters. A little research goes a long way toward deciding where you want to tour and planning it out in advance.

The next few chapters should help you out with that. But before we get into that, I want to leave the newer riders with some advice, and some insight into what might be called the "touring rider's frame of mind." Whether we consciously acknowledge it or not—and for most of us it simply goes without saying—all of the priorities listed above, as important as they might be, are usually not considered until our first priority is met—for myself and many other touring riders, that's taking the road less traveled.

To me, there is nothing better than riding down a little-used road that goes nowhere in particular. Here is where you will always find the most interesting little towns, shops, and restaurants. Not to mention such roads keep you away from most traffic, and most notably, those dreaded motorhomes. Still, whenever possible, it is usually best to first do a little research about road conditions. Checking with the highway department in advance isn't a bad idea, but it is even easier and more informative simply to stop at a local gas station or restaurant and ask a local. Most of the time they're happy to help and will often clue you in about little-known detours or things to see along the way. This can be one of the best parts about touring the road less traveled.

Part of the fun of motorcycle touring is sharing the experience with the one you love.

The Road Less Traveled

I suppose it goes without saying that, as motorcyclists, we tend to favor traveling on the kinds of roads that most people would prefer to avoid. In some ways, that works to our favor because it gets us away from the bulk of traffic. In other ways it often works against us, since such roads often tend not to lead to anywhere we might actually be headed. Luckily for us we are, for the most part, also the kind of people who place a higher priority on the journey than on the destination. I've yet to hear a motorcyclist complain about how long it took him to get where he was going, unless he'd traveled there by some means other than on his bike. I know I'll bitch to high heaven if I have to sit on an airplane for six or seven hours to get somewhere, or drive more than an hour to get anywhere. And yet, when I'm on my bike, I'll purposely look for a route that extends my journey as long as possible. I'm sure you've all heard your riding friends brag at one time or another: "Yep. The map said it was 120 miles from home to here, but I managed to ride 380 miles. Took me all day to get here—isn't that great?" You've made that boast yourself a time or two, haven't you? And admit it: you then gloried in explaining the intricacies of the convoluted route you put together, and how great the riding was along the way.

I often find it "necessary," sometimes with only the thinnest of excuses, to ride across the Mojave Desert on my way to Las Vegas, Phoenix, or other destinations east of California. I've developed a half-dozen different ways to accomplish such journeys, not counting the one or two that would be most obvious to non-riders. One of my favorites involves some almost abandoned stretches of the original Route 66, plus a couple of roads that don't even appear on most maps. Along the way, I come within sight—which out in the

Continued on page 91

A lack of planning ahead can lead to situations like this, where the road is closed for construction and the nearest detour is 150 miles out of your way. If you're the tour leader, you might have a bit of a problem winning everyone's trust back.

Parable:
Your Own Backyard

Recently, I was leading the tenth anniversary Readers' Tour for **Friction Zone** magazine, headed back to the coast after visiting six national parks in Utah. On the last day, we cut across the Mojave Desert on a series of my favorite old backroads: Nipton, Cima, Morningstar Mine, and Kelbaker roads, with a stopover at the old Kelso-Cima train depot, which was recently renovated by the National Park Service.

While visiting the museum there, and viewing the Kelso Sand Dunes, **Friction Zone**'s editor, Amy Holland, remarked that she'd never ridden this route and wanted me to show her just where

We all daydream about travelling to the far corners of the planet. While you should ride the Kamchatka Peninsula if the opportunity arises, oftentimes some of the best riding might be right in your backyard.

One of the great advantages of touring on a motorcycle is that you actually experience the world around you; you get to not just see it, but experience its smells and sounds as well.

we were on a map. Quite frankly I was surprised, because as I told her, "Amy, if you just follow this road on across the Mojave National Preserve, you'll connect with Highway 62 in Twentynine Palms, which will take you to the base of the Pines to Palms Highway, and straight on to your house, in only a couple of hours!"

In essence, we were right in her own backyard, and though she'd ridden a motorcycle literally coast

to coast on more than one occasion, and crossed the Mojave dozens of times, she never knew this route even existed. Like 99 percent of the travelers who crossed this desert—and there are over three million vehicles that do so each and every week— she'd always used the two interstate highways, believing them to be the fastest and easiest, if not the only way to navigate from Southern California to Las Vegas, Nevada. In truth, I've carefully plotted and ridden both ways many times, and though the

One great advantage of a tankbag is that it will have a map pocket. Pick a spot on that map and ride there. Chances you will see something you've never seen before.

back way is a bit more circuitous, the actual travel time is only 10 minutes longer, and that's if traffic on the highways is light, which it almost never is.

In addition, the scenery is definitely better, and it's simply much less stressful not to have to deal with all those giant semi-trucks and the half-crazed partygoers who just can't wait to get to Vegas to lose their money. Americans are so tuned-in to using interstate highways that they simply don't consider going off on backroads, which was evidenced by the fact that when we crossed under the two interstates, each had thousands of cars and trucks on it, running almost bumper to bumper, and yet on our route, we saw about one vehicle every 10 or 15 minutes, if that.

Along the way we passed through or alongside the world's largest Joshua Tree forest, lava flows, extinct volcanoes, salt flats, and one of the largest sand dune fields in North America, made even rarer by the fact it's only one of two or three such sites in the world with singing dunes, which make sounds like a giant pipe organ when the wind blows over them—all things that the interstate travelers, just a few miles away, would never know existed.

I would like to think that motorcyclists, for the most part, are immune to this phenomenon, but I'm afraid the truth is just the opposite. Though there's definitely a large segment within motorcycling that makes a point of avoiding the most direct or quickest line of travel and instead looks for the out-of-the-way routes, it seems the majority carry their four-wheeled driving habits over to their motorcycling, and that's a crying shame.

A GPS can prove an invaluable tool for long-distance touring, but it has a tyrannical side as well. GPS units are programmed to find routes that are fast and convenient; they don't place much value on scenic beauty, and often the most out-of-the-way routes are also the most scenic.

And then there are people like Amy, who've spent years traveling long distances specifically to seek out interesting places and little-known roads, but who tend to revert back to the highway mentality when close to home. I can't tell you how many times I've been traveling somewhere halfway across the country, or even the world, to ride some great roads and visit some interesting places, only to encounter local riders along the way who freely admitted they'd never seen the places I was going to visit. Not too long ago, I met a rider from Brazil who was exploring our Sierra Nevada Mountains, and having a hell of a good time. In talking to him, I found he was from a small city I'd visited a few years ago, and I mentioned that it must be great living so close to the Graciosa Trail, one of the world's best motorcycling roads, which I'd traveled for weeks to visit and to ride. To my surprise, he noted that he'd never ridden the Trail, though it was less than three hours from his house. And yet, he'd traveled many thousands of miles to ride in our North American mountains. Does that make sense?

When I met my wife, Cherrie, she'd lived in Colorado for her entire life and yet had never seen Pike's Peak, Rocky Mountain National Park, the Great Sand Dunes, or the Royal Gorge, all of which were mere day trips from her home of over 20 years. An even more egregious example of this syndrome occurred when we moved to Connecticut for two years. I was asked by the dealership I worked for to organize some weekend rides for our sponsored riding club. Not knowing the area at all, I procured several guidebooks from the Connecticut Department of Tourism, read them through, and then went riding, trying out different

If you live in the mountains or near an ocean, chances are you know about the scenic beauty in your region. But even if you don't live in an area considered scenic, odds are that there is something worth seeing not too far away.

out-of-the-way routes to string together a group of the more interesting sites in the area. I put together three such weekend rides, which were well-attended by local riders, nearly all of whom had lived in the area their entire lives. In fact, I recall several of them telling me they were fourth- and fifth-generation residents in the same little towns and villages, tracing their family lineage back to the Revolutionary War. I felt wholly unprepared and inadequate to show these people the roads and history of the area their own forefathers had settled, and yet was amazed to find that over half of them had never ridden the roads I took them on, nor seen the historical sites we visited! Several of them had taken extended motorcycle tours of Europe, Canada, and even South America, and yet they were unfamiliar with some of the great exploring available right in their own backyard.

This tendency has nothing at all to do with your personal sense of adventure, or your dedication to riding and exploring. It's a phenomenon that can easily be found in the most ardent of motorcycle

travelers. Call it a blind spot if you will, one that makes us tend to think that the best roads to travel and the best places to see are only those that require riding long distances over extended periods of time.

Try doing what I did in New England—get yourself a tourism guidebook for your area and see what the experts recommend as the best places to see in your home state. You might be surprised to find a whole list of things you never knew existed, and a whole new world to explore, right out your own back door.

If you prefer to take the path less traveled, it helps to have a traveling partner who shares your passion.

Continued from page 85

desert can mean as far away as 10 or 15 miles—of two different interstate highways. Sometimes I actually stop at the side of the road, just to gaze over at the interstate in wonder, looking at a line of bumper-to-bumper traffic that stretches back over the horizon more than 50 miles away. Even after over three decades of seeing this phenomenon, I'm amazed to think that here I am, with an open road stretching nearly 100 miles ahead and behind me, on which there probably aren't a dozen vehicles passing by in any given hour, and yet those thousands of lemmings wouldn't dream of going this way. And believe me, I am eternally grateful for their ignorance.

Finding the road less traveled is much more difficult out here in the Southwest than it was during the two years I spent in New England. Up in the quiet corner of Connecticut where I lived, there were literally thousands of miles of fabulous little two-lane back roads that could be used to get you almost anywhere you wanted to go, so long as you weren't in any great hurry to get there. I envy the New Englanders for that. Now, if we could just find some way to combine their Northeastern roads with our Southwestern weather, then we'd really have motorcycling nirvana!

The European Alpine regions offer perhaps the greatest compilation of lesser-traveled roads, in the smallest geographical area, of any place on earth. That's what

GPS or not, carrying a good old-fashioned road map is always a good idea. That is, unless you have too many leaders.

makes this one of the most treasured of all motorcycling destinations. Of course, it wasn't planned this way—it just sort of developed over the centuries. The original routes over the mountains were developed by the Romans both for trade and military purposes, and later on Napoleon built routes through the region for the same reasons. These routes followed the terrain as closely as possible, since they didn't have things like bulldozers and giant earth-moving machines. Besides which, they didn't need to handle anything wider than two horses abreast, which also happens to be the perfect formula for developing a great motorcycling road.

Okay, so you don't speak German or Italian. Neither do I, but is there really any doubt what these signs mean? Traveling in a foreign country doesn't have to be any more stressful than you make it. Relax and enjoy the adventure!

But as both technology and traffic developed, newer, wider, and easier to travel routes were developed, often employing tunnels and bridges, bypassing and replacing the centuries-old Roman and Napoleonic routes. Nowadays, most of the Alpine passes can be avoided with these newer roads, leaving the older, longer, narrower, and much more time-consuming routes open almost strictly for tourists and localized traffic. With the exception of the occasional tourist bus, these roads are now virtually private playgrounds for bicyclists and motorcyclists.

But as great a riding venue as the Alps are, you probably noticed that in my personalized rating system, the Alps came in second to my all-time favorite touring destination: New Zealand. There's a very simple reason for that, which can be distilled to one word: traffic. New Zealand is one of the least-populated countries in the world, and even better, most of that population is concentrated in four major cities, meaning that the thousands of miles of backroads that crisscross the islands are virtually devoid of traffic of any kind. Considering that New Zealand is the only place I've ever experienced that would rate a perfect "10" in this category and a "9" in all the other categories; it comes as close to being a perfect place to tour on a motorcycle as any place on earth, in my own humble opinion.

Of course, for most of us, touring such exotic locales as New Zealand or the Alps is something we might only get the opportunity to experience once or twice in a lifetime, if at all. The majority of our touring is going to be in our own country, and perhaps even in our own state. These rides, while perhaps not

You'll find that many European countries are very friendly toward people traveling on motorcycle.

Of course there are always road signs . . .

If you travel with other people, add extra time when planning your route for things like unscheduled breaks and bathroom stops.

quite as exciting, can be just as satisfying, but I still see many riders missing out on the opportunities presented so close to their own homes, as described in the following story.

Managing Time and Distance

Recently, during a four-day ride around the Southwest, my riding companion noted that he was somewhat amazed at my ability to accurately estimate each day's riding schedule in advance. So long as we left at or near the planned time in the morning, we would make our destination that evening at almost exactly the time I'd predicted, despite taking routes neither of us had ridden before and making unplanned rest stops and such.

Actually, there's no great mystery to this—it's mostly just a matter of practice and experience. When you've been touring for nearly 40 years, you develop a pretty good sense of time and distance, and can automatically factor in a number of criteria almost without thinking about it. Of course, these days I have an awful lot of high-tech assistance from my computer mapping programs and my GPS. But I've also learned that even computers and GPS systems are only as smart as the information they get from you, and aren't totally reliable. For example, if I plug in a destination and my GPS says I'll arrive there in five hours, I know immediately that I need to add two hours to that arrival time if I'm riding alone, and three hours if I'm leading a group. That's because even

The Honda Gold Wing was the first bike to have an integrated, built-in GPS system, as shown here. At first I thought, "What a great idea!" But I no longer believe that. I had a GL with "Navi," as they call it, and learned to hate it very quickly. Though having a large, bright screen built into the dash was great, everything else about the system drove me nuts. First and foremost, the unit cannot be removed and taken into the house to be hooked up to my computer for late nights of plotting and uploading routes. In fact, the only way to plot a route on the integrated GPS is to sit on the bike, with the key on, using the clumsy fairing-mounted controls to work the onscreen keyboard. That takes about 10 times longer than it would on my computer, and worst of all, the GPS won't store the routes for future use. It also means that upgrading your software or map programs requires you to take the bike into a dealership instead of doing it yourself. Add to that the fact that if you ever want to upgrade to a newer GPS unit, you are totally out of luck. Both of my current bikes have add-on GPS mounts, one by the factory and one I did myself. My GPS can be switched from bike to bike, or even to my car, and I recently upgraded to a newer version without having to change a thing. I love it.

though the GPS is smart enough to factor in changes in speed due to different types of roads, or urban congestion and such, it always assumes a constant rate of forward travel. There are no provisions for bad weather, rest stops, gas stops, or short layovers to read a historical marker or take a photo or two. And the time factor for each of these can be increased by around three to four extra minutes for each extra bike in the group. Riding by myself, a stop for gas and the restroom will probably take about 10 minutes. But if I'm leading a group of 30 riders on 17 bikes, as I've been known to do, that same gas-and-potty stop is going to consume around an hour—if I'm lucky and don't have any dawdlers.

Of course, I could pre-program the GPS with the stops, and estimated the time for each, but I prefer to be able to adjust those on the fly according to how things are going that day with weather and road conditions, the attitude of the group, and other variables. With the route programmed to go straight through to the end from wherever and whenever I am right now, I can easily see how much "fudge time" I have between the GPS ETA and the actual time I need to get in, and adjust future stops accordingly.

> ℱlexibility is always a key factor in motorcycle touring, even to the point of having several alternate routes branching off from your original, in case of accidents, bad weather, or brushfires — each of which have forced me to reroute a tour at least once.

I'd rather be able to do that myself than to have the system already locked to a specific stop and start time. Flexibility is always a key factor in motorcycle touring, even to the point of having several alternate routes branching off from your original, in case of accidents, bad weather, or brushfires—each of which have forced me to reroute a tour at least once.

Over the years I've tried out just about every computerized mapping system available to make advance plans for tours. Each has it own advantages and disadvantages, but overall, I decided a long time ago that Microsoft's Streets and Trips works best for me, mostly because it has the most flexibility in customizing my profile according to the speeds that I choose for different types of roads. It also allows me to prioritize the type of roads I want to ride on a sliding scale. Unlike in so many other systems, including the ones built into most GPS units, instead of having to choose whether interstate highways are allowed or omitted, I can rate them on a preference scale from 0 to 100 percent, and the program will allow or omit them accordingly when plotting my final route. Streets and Trips also allows me to customize my starting and stopping times, and will automatically factor in rest stops at whatever intervals I choose throughout the day, for whatever duration; I can say "Factor a 10-minute rest stop every 2 hours," or I can set up specific times and places for things like lunch and dinner, all very easily. Once you've used this program a few times, and learned how to customize the defaults to your own riding style, you'll be amazed at how accurately it can plot your riding day.

All of that is the "fancy" way of doing things when planning a structured ride, but over the years I've found that for more casual trips, it's pretty easy to just look at a map, whether on paper or a computer screen, and after figuring how many miles I have to go that day, applying a simple formula: for every 60 miles of interstate, add one hour; for every 50 miles of state highway, add another hour; and add an hour for every 40 miles of back roads and another for every 20 miles of city streets. Believe it or not, that system works almost perfectly for figuring your total travel time for any given day. Of course there are exceptions and additions to the formula, such as interstate highways as they pass through major metropolitan areas. For those stretches, you need to drop your average by 10 mph, just as you do for state highways passing through cities, or even back roads passing through small towns. I know it sounds a bit complicated, but once you get the hang of it, it really isn't difficult at all.

Of all the things that newbies get wrong when starting out, I think the worst and most common is fixating on making a predetermined distance each day, to the exclusion of all else — including actually enjoying the ride.

I should note that in general, this little formula of mine only applies to North America. In South America, in general, all speeds can be increased by 5–10 mph (except in Mexico), and in many parts of Europe you can subtract 5–10 mph. In most European cities, you can subtract even more. You haven't seen traffic congestion until you've ridden in Madrid or Rome, and if you plan on riding in the Alps, you can throw the whole formula out the window. I once spent nearly a month riding through Germany, Austria, Switzerland, and Northern Italy, and found that if I averaged 30 mph during any given day, I was doing well. Not that the riding wasn't absolutely fabulous, but it's hard to imagine how incredibly narrow, twisty, and challenging the Alpine roads can be until you've actually ridden them. You'll also need rest stops considerably more often, simply because the mental and physical challenges of riding these roads are so much greater than what we Americans are accustomed to facing.

I realize that in the case of many of you, I'm preaching to the choir. If you've done much motorcycle touring, you've most likely developed your own system and your own set of criteria for managing time and distance when you tour. But I think it's important to remember that each summer, there's a whole new crop of riders just getting started in touring, and my hope is that some of this advice will help them avoid the common rookie pitfalls of planning their first tours. Of all the things that newbies get wrong when starting out, I think the worst and most common is fixating on making a predetermined distance each day, to the exclusion of all else—including actually enjoying the ride. When they're just getting started, they tend to think of time and mileage in the terms they're most familiar with, which is driving a car. As a result, they end up pushing too hard, exhausting themselves, and not enjoying the ride nearly so much as they could have had they simply reduced their time and mileage expectations.

If you're anything like me, this is your idea of paradise.

Chapter 5

Packing

What you might pack to take along on a tour is one of those very personal things that will vary greatly from one person to the next. However, that doesn't mean that there aren't some general guidelines that might help you prioritize the use of your packing space. This chapter will help accelerate your learning curve so that you don't have to go through quite so long a period of trial and error as many riders have (like myself, for example). Almost inevitably, by the end of a tour, or a series of tours, you'll find that there are certain things you've been carrying that were completely useless and just taking up space, and other things you wished you'd brought along but neglected to pack.

The integrated saddlebags of the Gold Wing are among the best in the world: spacious, waterproof, and easy to access. Their only drawback is the latching system, which is built into the frame in such a way that it often gets jammed up with your luggage.

To keep it simple, we'll separate our items into three basic categories: clothing, personal items, and safety and emergency items.

Clothing

By far the majority of your packing space will be taken up with clothing, though this is somewhat less true if you ride solo, and a bit more true if you're touring two-up. I believe it's also true that it's in this category that we see the most problems with overpacking (see the section on overpacking for a more detailed discussion). My rule of thumb, though it might seem overly austere to most, is to carry two basic off-bike outfits, one for "warm and dry," and one for "cold and wet." To this I add two or three changes of socks and underwear, and figure I can always take an hour or two out somewhere along the way to do a quick load of laundry, if necessary. Other options and adjustments to this system include washing out my underwear in the sink of the hotel room, or even packing old, worn underwear, throwing it out when it gets dirty, and purchasing a cheap three-pack of socks or briefs at the next Wal-Mart or K-Mart I pass. I've found that more often than not, you can actually replace such items at a discount store

The Givi-style top case used by BMW and many other bike makers has pretty much become the standard in the industry. They come in a multitude of sizes, are very durable and waterproof, are easily removable, and have a latching system outside of the packing area so they don't jam up in your gear.

for cheaper than you can wash and dry them at a laundromat, and a whole lot quicker.

Shoes tend to take up an inordinate amount of space, so I long ago settled on one of two options, depending on the climate conditions where I'm riding. If I'm traveling through a more or less temperate climate zone, I carry only a pair of webbed sandals. This not only minimizes my need for socks, but the sandals compress a bit more than shoes and usually can be jammed into one of those odd-shaped corners of a saddlebag or trunk where not much else will fit. In addition, if it does get a bit chilly, you can still wear a pair of socks with them. But if the area I'm riding through tends to be a bit colder or wetter, such as touring through Nova Scotia, then I carry a pair of deck shoes—those lightweight, tennis shoe-like footwear favored by boaters. These again can be compressed to a certain degree for packing in odd-shaped spaces, but are a bit warmer, somewhat waterproof, and more socially acceptable for wearing into restaurants than the sandals might be.

Personal Items

The majority of your personal items will go into a small toiletries bag, preferably one that's waterproof, in case something leaks. It probably goes without saying that each item should be as small as is practical. For example, you certainly don't want to carry a 16-ounce bottle of shampoo or sunscreen. Items like that should be purchased in small, unbreakable travel sizes, which can easily be found at almost any discount store or pharmacy. Always remember that the key is size and weight.

Checking my own bag, I find the following items:

- *Shampoo*
- *Nail clippers and file*
- *Two small packets of laundry soap*
- *Sunscreen*
- *Antacids*
- *Tiny eyeglass repair kit*
- *Disposable razor*
- *Hand soap*
- *Two sets of contact lenses*
- *Painkillers (for headache, sore muscles, etc.)*
- *Eyedrops*
- *Comb*
- *Toothbrush and toothpaste*

All of that fits into a nylon bag about eight inches wide and three inches deep, which can be carried in a little corner nook in one of my saddlebags where nothing else will fit, much like the shoes and sandals. Naturally your own list will probably vary somewhat, but this should give you a basic starting point.

I asked my wife to check her bag, to see if there were any extra things she might carry that I don't, and her list added:

- **Cream rinse**—Because she has very long hair, and despite her best efforts in braiding and tying it up, it gets very tangled by the end of the day.

- **Rubbing alcohol**—She likes to carry the alcohol pads, saying she can use them to clean her jewelry, and that they're also good to have around in case you need to disinfect a small cut or insect bite.

- **Hair dryer**—For the same reason as the cream rinse, but at least she was able to find a small, portable unit that folds up. I fought this at first, but have to admit it has also come in very handy for drying out gloves and such after getting caught in the rain.

- **Makeup and makeup remover towelettes**—Though she never wears makeup when we're riding, because it comes off on the helmet lining and makes an awful mess, she likes to get gussied up a bit for going out to dinner some evenings. Here again, I've found alternative uses for the towelettes. When we're traveling in the desert, they come in real handy during the day for wiping the grime off your face, not to mention cooling you off and generally refreshing yourself at a rest stop.

- **Small hand mirror**—This is another of those things I initially complained about, since the hotel rooms or the campground facilities always have mirrors, but I've found it handy at times for reasons other than hers. In particular, a common problem encountered when touring is getting some kind of foreign particle in one of your eyes, despite your best efforts to avoid it. When that happens, a moist towelette and small mirror (particularly one like my wife carries, which magnifies) can be invaluable for removing the offending grit immediately. After all, it's not the sort of problem you can leave until the end of the day, or even the next gas stop.

Safety and Emergency Items

Not too long ago, I was giving a presentation on my motorcycle tours to a group of riders at Bob's BMW in Jessup, Maryland. At the end, we had a question-and-answer session, and one of the guys asked me what kind of "extra" things he should carry along on a week-long tour that he wouldn't normally pack for a day trip.

I have to admit, my first reaction was that other than extra clothes, there wasn't really any difference. But then I realized I was looking at the problem from my own perspective, as a professional tourer, and not looking at it from his perspective. After asking him a few questions, and finding that he'd never strayed from home for more than a weekend on his bike, it began to dawn on me that he probably never considered carrying the kind of gear that's "normal" for someone like me (and probably a lot of you). So I mentally reviewed my list of touring essentials, then deducted the things that most riders would carry pretty much all of the time (like a cell phone or a digital camera), and came up with the following list of my ten touring essentials. I'm sure most of you can come up with other items, but these are what came to mind when doing a mental inventory of my bike's contents just before leaving on a tour. At the risk of ripping off the Boy Scouts, it's always best to be prepared.

Rainsuit

I suppose it depends on where you live and ride as to whether or not you'd normally keep a rainsuit on your bike, but here in the Southwest, most of us don't think about such things very often. However, if you're going out for a week-long tour, especially through an area unfamiliar to you, you really don't want to be caught without one. For years I've carried nothing but Frogg Toggs, simply because they allow air to pass through so you don't sweat like a pig when wearing them, and they pack up really small. And even if I'm riding in an area where I might get chilled when wet, I figure I can always put insulated gear on underneath them. Of course, in colder, wetter climates, instead of wearing my mesh riding suit, I'll wear an insulated, two-piece suit that's also waterproof, which negates the need for bringing along a rainsuit. The only problem with such suits is that if you encounter warm, dry weather, they can be extremely uncomfortable, which is why I usually opt for the mesh suit, as it gives me more options.

Earplugs and Carrier

I know that a lot of people who only go out for a day ride don't bother with earplugs, but again, if you're going on a tour, they're an essential that shouldn't be ignored. Unfortunately, I learned that truth late in my riding career, and I now suffer from tinnitus, and about 30 percent irreversible hearing loss as a result. Still, even after getting educated, I had a problem with never having a spare set of earplugs around if I lost one, or if they simply got too dirty or damaged to use. And then someone at Kawasaki gave me a great little waterproof earplug case that attaches to your jacket's zipper pull with a chain. I make a point of stashing one or two spare pair of earplugs in the case just before leaving on a trip. They stay clean and dry, and I always know where they are when I need them. Since then, I've found similar little cases at most pharmacies, though they don't look as cool as my bright green Kawasaki one. Though I use disposable earplugs (with a sound-reducing quality of at least 30 decible [dB]), there is no doubt that custom-molded ones do a better job of protecting your hearing. I've owned two sets like that and loved them, but I tend to lose things pretty easily, and misplaced both pairs, even when they had those cords for hanging them around your neck. Don't ask me how I did it, because I don't know.

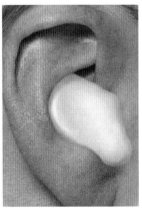

Emergency Funds

Did you ever think of what might happen if your wallet and/or credit cards got lost or stolen while you were a couple thousand miles from home? Of course, you can usually find a bank or even a friend to help you out in such an emergency, but wouldn't things be a lot easier and less stressful if you just had a hidden stash of some kind? I usually keep one extra credit card (that isn't used for anything else), and about $200 in cash, sealed in a waterproof freezer bag and secured somewhere away from my regular belongings. Naturally

Would you believe this is in the middle of the Mojave Desert? It was the first snowstorm in this area in over 25 years, but it just goes to prove that you never know what you're going to encounter on a tour. Thank goodness I was carrying my heated vest.

I'm not going to tell you where, in case you see my bike parked somewhere sometime and decide to play a nasty little practical joke on Uncle Fred, but you get the idea.

Flashlight with Charger

I used to keep a small flashlight stashed in my saddlebags, trunk, or tankbag, but it seemed every time I actually needed it, the batteries would be dead. Then my friend Marc gave me a gift for Christmas a couple of years ago that has now become one of my touring essentials. It's a small flashlight with four very bright LED bulbs, and a collapsible crank that turns an internal generator to charge it up. One minute of cranking gives you four minutes of light, and it also has a plug on the end with six different adaptors, so it can be used to recharge cell phones, iPods, or any number of other, battery-powered devices. I love it, and it has really come in handy more than once out on the road, if for nothing more than reading a map when I get hopelessly lost in the middle of the night (*sans* GPS, of course).

Swiss Army Knife or Multitool

I shouldn't have to explain the thousands of jobs these little gadgets can accomplish for you. I carry both: a small Swiss Army knife in my pocket and a Leatherman multitool in the bike. I've used them over the years to pull a splinter from my hand, shape a tire plug, fix a broken zipper, rewire a taillight, and even hot-wire an ignition when I lost my key once, which brings us to essential number six ...

Spare Bike Key

Once, in Arkansas, I lost my bike key. I won't tell you how—it's much too degrading. Besides, it's one of my wife's favorite stories to relate when she wants to embarrass me. But the bottom line is, I lost it. I've also had friends lose keys while on tour, and depending on where it happens, or even what day of the week it is, it can take up to three days just to get a replacement, and that can totally ruin your tour. These days I keep a spare, wrapped up in electrical tape and secured somewhere on the bike frame that's not too easy to access. Of course I've never had to use one since I started doing this, but I see it as a kind of karmic insurance—you know, like if you carry a rainsuit it won't rain, and that sort of thing.

Hiding a spare key somewhere on the bike can prevent embarrassing situations.

Wee Willy

Okay, so you're probably asking yourself what the heck a Wee Willy is. These days there are lots of imitations that go by other names, but I believe the original pocket-sized windshield/faceshield cleaner system was the old Wee Willy. Simply put, it's a small plastic bottle with a little spray pump on top. It also has a soft sponge attached to one side of the bottle, and a short length of squeegee (probably cut from a windshield wiper blade) attached to the other side. You fill the bottle with a couple of ounces of water, then add a drop or two of dishwashing soap. Shake it up a little to mix and drop it into your pocket. Now when you stop for gas or for a cool drink at a rest stop, you just pull out your Wee Willy, spritz some cleaner on your bug-encrusted windshield and/or faceshield, then work it around with the sponge. Once it looks like you've broken all the guts and grime loose from the surface, spin the bottle around and squeegee the surface clean. Voila!

Extra Sunglasses

I suppose this doesn't seem important enough to put on this list, as you can pick up a cheap pair of sunglasses at almost any gas station, but hear me out. I think we can all agree that sunglasses are a touring essential, and that carrying a spare pair is probably a pretty good idea. But the main reason for listing them is that if you should actually need your spare pair, I think it's a real bad idea to have to get by with whatever you can find on the road. I've seen a friend suffer a serious eye injury when a small rock struck his sunglasses, simply because they weren't shatterproof; I've come very close to a bad accident myself as a result of using polarized sunglasses. I know, I know—polarized lenses are supposed to reduce glare and be good for riding, but I found a real bad downside to using them. You see, a lot of bikes have windshields or instrument panels made from Lexan plastic, not to mention its common use in helmet faceshields. And under certain conditions, when the sun is at the

right angle, if you're wearing polarized sunglasses, your windshield or faceshield may suddenly, without warning, either turn totally black or explode in a rainbow spectrum of bright colors that you can't see through. This usually happens at the worst possible time, and carries potentially deadly consequences. Trust me—get some decent, shatterproof, non-polarized sunglasses, and an extra pair to stow away while on tour.

First-Aid Kit and Tire Repair Kit
I'm lumping these two together because they're virtual no-brainers for any touring rider, but then again, I don't think most day trippers bother with either. Getting a flat tire a couple of blocks, or even a couple of miles from your home or place of work, is usually not a big deal. But the last time I had one, I was 90 miles from the nearest town, in the middle of the Mojave Desert. Suddenly a tire repair kit made a lot of sense, particularly one that's simple to use and effective, and carries a means of re-inflating the tire, whether by pump or by CO_2 cartridges. And if you think it might be dicey to be lose air in your tires 100 miles out in the desert, imagine losing blood instead! Even a small cut can be serious if you're not prepared to disinfect it and stop the bleeding almost immediately. A small first-aid kit is cheap insurance against ruining your tour.

Continued on page 114

Parable:

The Turnkey Tourer

Sit back children, and let the old man tell you a tale of the good old days of motorcycle touring.

Back then (let's say around 1970), when I prepared for a ride of any duration, it meant packing all my emergency gear. That included a spare inner tube and patch kit, a small air pump, a can of chain lube, a master link, a chain-breaker tool, tire irons, a couple of spark plugs, and an assortment of extra tools to complement the regular toolkit that came with the bike (something you hardly ever see anymore). These usually included wire cutters, Vise-Grips, a plug gap tool, and feeler gauges. To round things out, I would purchase a spare throttle cable and spare clutch cable. Each would be routed alongside the in-service cable and tied into place with wiring ties. That way, if a cable broke on the road,

even at night in the middle of nowhere, I could pretty easily unscrew the ends of the old cable and screw on the new one. It would be enough to get me to civilization, where I could then remove the old cable and adjust the new one to work properly.

My kit also included a spare headlight bulb and taillight bulb, and a handful of fuses and butt-end wire splicers, along with a tube of epoxy. I would've carried a fire extinguisher too, if I could've found room for it. More than once it would've saved me

Aerostich sells an excellent toolkit that includes virtually everything you'd ever need on a motorcycle trip.

a lot of heartache. The problem is, no matter how carefully you plan for disaster, fate always has an extra trick or two up its sleeve.

If that seems like an awful lot of over-preparation to you, you're probably younger than 40. If it seems like barely enough, you're probably over 60. In truth, I used every one of those items at least once, and the carrying of each was predicated on having once been stranded for its lack. In fact, on some later, longer tours, I also carried a breaker plate, consisting of a set of ignition points and a condenser, and a miniature set of homemade jumper cables, not to mention a flashlight and a spare set of batteries for it.

The Aerostich toolkit rolls up into a convenient pouch so it doesn't take up much space in your luggage.

Anal, you say? Paranoid? Maybe, but you should know that today I've been known to head off for a month's ride through the Amazon rainforest with much less preparation. The reason is very simple: the machines have improved that much in the ensuing years. My last wiring fire occurred in 1983, and I hardly ever ride a bike anymore that has tubes in the tires, ignition points, a chain, or even cables for the clutch and brakes.

Some people, especially some my own age, will argue that this is a bad thing—that, for example, at least when your points closed up you could take off the cover, adjust them with a screwdriver, and get back on the road. Nowadays, if an electronic ignition goes out on the road, you have no hope but a tow truck. There's a certain amount of truth in that kind of thinking, but I'll also argue that the newer technologies that replaced the fairly easily fixable ones also break down with much less frequency. Sure, chain drives are more mechanically efficient and more easily repaired than a shaft drive system, but I dare you to show me a chain that has

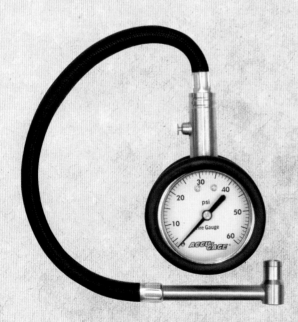

Even the most reliable modern bike has tires that need pressurized air to remain inflated, and atmospheric conditions have an effect on pressurized air. Because of this you will need a reliable air pressure gauge.

operated flawlessly for over 150,000 miles like my last shaft drive did. And I didn't have to lube and adjust it several times a week, or listen to my wife complain on tour when it splattered fresh oil all over her pants leg.

I rode through the bad old days of Lucas (aka "Prince of Darkness") electrics, and once toured across the Rockies (off-road) on a Hodaka that would foul out its spark plug about every 150 to 200 miles. I carried several spark plugs in each jacket pocket, and routinely replaced them with every

gas fill-up, if they lasted that long. The practice of routing a spare clutch cable in place began when the one on my Honda CB750 broke in the middle of Utah, in the middle of the night, about 100 miles from the nearest town. Luckily, at the time I'd already gotten in the habit of carrying a set of Vise-Grips, so I attached them to the broken cable end and wedged them against the tank with my left knee. To shift, I would let go of the left handlebar, grab the Vise-Grips, and yank upward while I let off the throttle with my right hand and shifted with my left foot. It wasn't pretty, but it worked.

Today's motorcycles are infinitely more reliable than those produced a couple of generations ago, but anything mechanical is subject to mechanical failure. It's still a good idea to carry at least a basic toolkit.

Back in those days, you could pretty much identify a motorcyclist by the grease under his fingernails. Some guys really enjoyed the mechanical interaction that the sport entailed, and some, like me, hated it, but were willing to endure it as the price we paid for the joy of riding.

All that's in the past now. I can hardly remember the last time a bike gave me any serious trouble—but then again, my definition of serious trouble is definitely colored by my past, and considerably different from that of more contemporary riders. The other day, I listened to a guy bitch for over half an hour about his new Honda Gold Wing, on which he'd just returned from a two-week vacation. His major complaint was that when he rode at under 15 mph, the temperature gauge would run into the red zone. I asked him if the bike ever actually overheated, spit up its coolant, or refused to run. "No," he said, "but that's not the point. I paid $23,000 for that piece of junk, and it shouldn't DO that!" On further questioning, I found that during his 3,500-mile trip, the overheating had only occurred for about 2 miles, but again he insisted that I was missing the point. After which, to support his claim that the bike was "a piece of junk," he regaled me with another tale of how, just to add insult to injury, his multiple CD changer had jammed. Horrors! To hear him talk, the bike had ruined his entire vacation, and Honda owed him a brand-new replacement machine.

Evidently, I'm getting really, really old.

My grandfather rode this 1914 Excelsior Super Ace all over the country, performing all repairs and maintenance with a handful of tools he carried in his jacket pockets. Once, by his own account, he fashioned a main bearing for the engine from a tobacco tin and installed it by the light of his campfire using a pocketknife, screwdriver, and pair of pliers. It still runs today, by the way—nearly 100 years later. Now, look at the new Concours 14 on the facing page. Can you imagine even replacing a spark plug without taking it into the shop?

Continued from page 109

Packing For International Touring

Preparing for an international tour requires a bit more thought than a domestic tour, and packing along certain items you might not normally carry with you. This list is going to vary a great deal depending on where you're going, how long you're staying, and a number of other factors, but there are certain items that would almost always be a good idea to have along, and it's only those that we're going to cover here. I have divided these items into three basic categories: documents, insurance, and personal items.

Documents

The first and most important document you can carry is your passport, but there are several items in regard to your passport that you should attend to. First, check the expiration date, and make sure it doesn't fall within six months of your scheduled trip. Different countries have different rules regarding foreign passports, but one of the most common is that they might require that your passport not expire within three to four months of your planned exit from their country. If it does expire in that timeframe, they might refuse you entrance until you can get a renewal, and that can sometimes take up to six weeks. Plan ahead, and apply for renewal at least a couple of months before you leave. Secondly, before leaving, make a high-quality, color copy of your passport, seal it in a waterproof bag, and stow it away someplace totally separate from your regular passport. If your passport is lost or stolen, having the duplicate copy to hand in at the local consulate will speed up the process of getting you an emergency visa or passport considerably. Often having the duplicate can save you as much as two or three days.

Normally, having a regular, state-issued driver's license from your home state will be quite sufficient in any kind of a traffic stop, rental, or accident situation. However, it's also true that many European, Asian, and South American countries are somewhat more bureaucratic and document-oriented than the U.S., and the more identification you can provide, the fewer hassles you'll have. For that reason, I carry both an International Driving License (IDL) and an International Driving Permit (IDP). These are very similar, only for different countries. The IDP is from the 1949 United Nations Convention on International Road Traffic, valid in all countries that signed the contract. It's easy and cheap to acquire simply by going to your local American Automobile Association (AAA) office, presenting your regular state license, having your picture taken, and paying a $10 fee. It takes about 15 minutes, and the fee is even waived if you're an AAA member.

Unfortunately, bureaucracies being what they are, a completely different license, the IDL, is required for most South American countries because we have a separate agreement with them, the Convention on Regulation of Inter-American Automotive Traffic. The IDL can be acquired in exactly the same way, and even at the same time as the IDP. Neither of these documents is essential, but either one might very well save you time and hassles in dealing with petty local bureaucrats, if for no other reason than the fact that you're demonstrating that you took the time and trouble to comply with their country's laws, rather than expecting them to extend you courtesy simply because you're a U.S. citizen.

Your valid U.S. passport is all you really need for travel almost anywhere, but should problems arise, such as a traffic accident or getting stopped for a minor traffic offense, I've found that securing local permits often smoothes things over considerably. The one on the left is an International Driving Permit, valid in almost all European countries, and the one on the right is an International Driving License, valid in most South American countries. Both can be secured through your local AAA office, with a small fee and your U.S. license (which, by the way, should always be presented along with the other permits).

Insurance

Most of us have several different types of insurance that will help out if something happens while on a tour, but if you're in a foreign country, you might find dealing with your insurance company to be a real problem. Not to mention that in most cases, whatever problem you're having is going to be one that you'll have to solve yourself, and pay for yourself. You'll have to deal with getting reimbursed after you get back home. Financially that may be okay with you, but in the meantime, your trip is ruined. Not to mention that the tour operator isn't going to give you back the money you paid for the tour upfront, which only makes sense, because he's spent your money already.

There are dozens if not hundreds of insurance companies that offer specialized trip insurance, and you need to at least consider availing yourself of their products. Typically, you can customize the degree of coverage you desire, opting for anything from tour cost reimbursement if anything prevents you from participating, to a comprehensive package deal that takes care of trip cancellation, trip interruption, medical expenses, lost luggage, and even a MedeVac service that will fly you back home in a sort of ambulance plane, if you're injured in such a manner that would require more than a day or two in a hospital. Comprehensive packages like this can vary in price from about $250 to $500 per person for a typical two-week overseas tour.

> There are dozens if not hundreds of insurance companies that offer specialized trip insurance, and you need to at least consider availing yourself of their products.

In reality, and in my own experience, the odds are about 200 to 1 that you won't need it, but for that 1 in 200, it can be a real lifesaver. Personally, I've taken the risk and not purchased such insurance, but on my most recent group tour to New Zealand, we had a couple along who had a motorcycle accident on the very first day of a 14-day tour, and missed out on all but the last three days. Besides losing all the money they'd spent for the tour, rooms, and meals, and the deductible on the damaged rental bike, they had to rent a car and get another room near the hospital for 10 days while the husband waited for the wife to have surgery done on her broken elbow. If they'd purchased the trip insurance package, they would've been reimbursed for over $12,000 in expenses. The decision is yours.

Personal Items

In addition to the normal personal items we discussed before, there are a few extra things you should consider when traveling out of the country. Probably the most important of these would be any medications you might be taking, but in addition, you really should have your doctor write out an extra prescription for you; carry it somewhere separate and safe, just like the copy of your passport. I'm a diabetic, and always carry my medicine with me, but on that same New Zealand tour I just mentioned, somehow I managed to lose my medication along the way. If I'd carried an extra prescription with me, any pharmacy would have been happy to sell me what I needed. But as it was, I had to make an emergency visit to a doctor and get a new prescription written before I could purchase what I needed. Don't make that same mistake.

The same caveat applies to eyeglasses and contact lenses. Sure, you should carry spares, but even those could get lost, and when you're 12,000 miles from home, in a foreign country where they might not speak your language, do you really want to take a day out of your tour to get an eye exam?

And finally, though these items aren't nearly as critical as they used to be, you should get yourself a set of universal electrical plug adaptors, and possibly even a voltage converter. Nowadays most electrical devices, like my laptop and my wife's hair dryer, have built-in voltage converters, so they can be used in almost any country in the world. Still, you should check to make sure they can handle variable voltages, and even if they can, odds are they come with only a North American-style

> Nowadays most electrical devices, like my laptop and my wife's hair dryer, have built-in voltage converters, so they can be used in almost any country in the world.

plug on the end of the cord. That being the case, you'll need at least one, and possibly several different plug configurations. Traveling through Europe, I believe I needed four different adapters. You can find these at almost any discount store like K-Mart or Wal-Mart, but I found my personal favorite at a Sharper Image store. While most universal adapter sets are rather bulky, mine packs up into a little box about three inches square, sort of like a kid's puzzle, and by disassembling it and reassembling in different configurations, it allows my plugs to work in any country in the civilized world.

Chapter 6

Choosing the Right Gear

Personal Accessories

Personal accessories, or riding gear, are the most difficult to define or to give advice about, simply because they're, well . . . so personal. No single riding jacket, or helmet, or pair of boots or gloves is going to be the most correct for all riders. The best we can hope to do here is to give you as much advice as possible to help you make the best decision in each category. While it might be true, for example, that no jacket is going to be the best for all riders, it's just as true that there are certain qualities and design criteria that are

The three best and most common types of touring helmets. From right to left: Full-face, modular (chin bar up), three-quarter, and another modular (chin bar down). Obviously, it was raining this day, and the only one with no face protection from it is the lady with the three-quarter helmet. Of course, she's a passenger, so it's not as critical for her to see as it is for the riders.

common among all good riding jackets, and you need to be cognizant of those when making your buying decision.

It's also true, and most unfortunate, that there's a great deal of misinformation floating about concerning such items, most of which is handed down from otherwise experienced riders. Undoubtedly some of the advice I'm about to give you is going to run counter to what you might have heard from other riders. When that happens, the best I can tell you is to use your own judgment, or do a little research. When in doubt, don't take anyone's advice, including mine, without checking out what you've been told. The Internet is a wealth of knowledge, so long as you take care to consider the source of the information you're getting. I think you'll get the idea of where I'm going with that advice as we go along, especially with our first item of riding gear, the helmet.

Helmets

Before we get into how to choose a helmet, let's make one thing perfectly clear: you should never ride without a quality helmet, approved by the Department of Transportation (DOT), fastened securely on your head, period. Despite any number of stories you might've heard about how a helmet can break your neck, block your vision, impair your hearing, or conjure up Satan, every single one of dozens of studies conducted around the world has consistently proven

otherwise. Riders who wear helmets are much less likely to be in accidents, and almost always suffer fewer and less severe injuries when they *are* involved in accidents. There really isn't any room for discussion on this, but even if common sense doesn't tell you it's true, feel free to check it out for yourself.

Helmets come in four basic styles: Full-coverage (full-face), modular (flip-up), three-quarter (open-face), and shorty (half-helmet). The level of protection provided by each is in that same order. A full-coverage helmet will give you the maximum amount of protection you can buy, which is exactly why you won't see professional racers wearing anything less. A modular helmet will come pretty close to providing the protection of a full-face model, while offering a bit more in the way of comfort and versatility for the touring rider. A three-quarter helmet will do an adequate job of protecting your skull, but does nothing to protect your face. Since accident studies show that over 25 percent of motorcycle accidents involve facial injuries, and about half of those facial injuries result in brain damage, you should really think twice about riding with an open-face, three-quarter helmet. The shorty, or half-helmet, is, quite frankly, a joke. While some actually meet the bare minimum standard under DOT guidelines, the majority of the ones you see are novelty helmets, actually

I was chased away from this vendor's booth when they saw me taking pictures because they knew they were selling illegal helmets and conning their customers. First of all, be wary of any helmet selling for $49—I don't believe it's possible to manufacture a quality safety helmet and sell if for that price. Second, the letters "DOT" stand for "Department of Transportation," and an oval, black-and-white sticker with these letters denotes that the manufacturer guarantees that their helmets have been subjected to and passed the tests for DOT safety certification. Obviously this guy got caught using fake DOT stickers, which can be purchased for about 99 cents each on the Internet. If you look closely at the helmet pictured, you can see the oval glue marks on the back, where the fake sticker used to be. After getting caught, and probably fined, this vendor simply peeled off the fake stickers and had the letters DOT painted on the helmet. There's no law against having the letters painted on the helmet, so long as they don't look like a DOT certification. The vendor is counting on you not knowing the difference, and he isn't about to mention it.

All motorcycle helmets are rated on four basic criteria:

Impact: the shock-absorbing capacity of the helmet

Penetration: the helmet's ability to withstand a blow from a sharp object without that object penetrating through to your head

Retention: the chin strap and chin strap locking mechanism's ability to stay fastened under impact without stretching or breaking

Peripheral vision: a design that allows a minimum of 105 degrees of side vision (normal human peripheral vision is only about 90 degrees)

A three-quarter helmet provides the least protection you should be willing to accept, but if you're going to ride with one, at least get a quality one like this, with good interior padding and top and back vents. Buy a visor (pictured) and a faceshield (not pictured) to go with it.

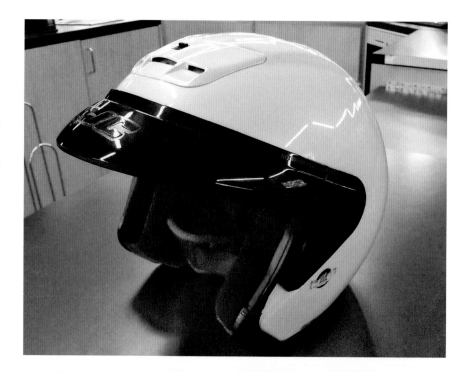

This fake helmet is virtually useless if this guy goes down, but in his defense, he really wants to ride without a helmet, which should be his right; the helmet is simply a protest against the law. If that's the way you feel, you have a right to it, but I don't want you to think that buying one of these pieces of crap is going to offer any kind of protection in an accident.

meant for use as part of a Halloween costume. Some people wear these as a protest against helmet laws, which is certainly their right—but don't let anyone try to tell you they're actually some kind of safety gear.

A helmet must meet the minimum standards in these four areas to pass the DOT certification and be allowed to carry the DOT sticker. And while I'll tell you here and now that you should never buy a helmet that doesn't carry that sticker, I must also warn you that it's all too easy to buy a counterfeit sticker and put it on a helmet. I've even seen the stickers for sale right out in the open at some motorcycle rallies. For that reason, you should always purchase your helmet from a reputable dealer, and stick to the known,

Once you think you've found a helmet you like, the most important thing to check is the fit.

major brands. The market is flooded with cheap imports, mostly from China, that have thin, inferior plastic shells, poor-quality Styrofoam liners, and chin straps so weak they can be broken loose with a hard pull from your bare hands. I know, because I've tried it and succeeded. For the most part, these helmets are sold over the Internet and by mail order, or are found at swap meets.

Once you think you've found a helmet you like, the most important thing to check is the fit. In truth, ill-fitting helmets cause many problems and can even contribute to injuries. But there are a few simple tests you can do to avoid these problems. First of all, the helmet needs to fit snugly on your head. There should be no gaps between the helmet liner and your temples or your forehead, and the cheek pads should press firmly, but not uncomfortably, against your cheeks. With the helmet secured on your head, you should be able to shake your head from side to side and up and down without the helmet moving on your head. If you grip the helmet with both hands and try to move it around, your skin should move with it. In addition, on full-face and modular helmets, place the palm of your hand flat against the chinbar and push it in firmly. If the chinbar touches any part of your nose or chin, you need a different design or a larger helmet. And finally, with the chin strap securely fastened, you should grip the rear lip of the helmet and try to roll it forward off your head. Try it until it hurts, then push a little harder. If you can roll the helmet off your head—even if it's painful to do so—the helmet is too large. Remember, if the impact of an accident can fling the helmet off your head, it isn't going to do you a darned bit of good.

After you've tried these tests, you need to leave the helmet on your head for at least 15 minutes. Walk around the dealership, looking around. Move your head up and down and back and forth in a normal manner. After 15 or 20 minutes, take the helmet off and see if you have any sore spots on your ears or head. No two helmets are going to fit you exactly the same, as no two heads are shaped exactly the same. You need to find one that's going to be comfortable when worn for as long as six hours a day, for several days in a row. An ill-fitting helmet will absolutely ruin your riding experience by inducing headaches and fatigue, and distracting your attention from the ride and the road.

Aerostich's Darien jacket is the industry standard for textile riding gear. These things will outlast even the most well-engineered motorcycle.

Jackets

Motorcycle jackets come in an enormous variety of materials and styles, and so, as with helmets, we're going to stick to the basics of what you need to look for in a quality riding jacket, though we'll divide some of that advice into the two most basic categories: leather and textiles. First of all, though, we need to talk about the important qualities that apply to boh: sizing, pockets, basic construction, collars, cuffs, closures, and liners.

Sizing

A riding jacket should be at least a bit loose, as there are times you'll want to put on heavier clothes under them or wear them with a liner of some kind. However, as with almost any advice of this kind, be careful not to go overboard. The amount of protection a jacket will give you is also related to how well it stays where it belongs when being abraded by a road surface. The easiest solution to this problem is to buy a jacket that has some kind of adjustability around the waist area, like a belt or zippers, and if possible, gaiters on the sleeves that allow you to tighten them against your arms. If you opt for a jacket with body armor this becomes even more important, as the belts and gaiters will insure that your armor is still covering your vital parts even after any initial impact.

Any true motorcycle jacket will fit you rather oddly when you're just walking around in it, because that's not what it's designed for. For example, when you're trying on the jacket in a store, with your arms at your sides, the sleeves should come down to about the knuckles on your fist, if not a bit farther. That's because when you're riding, with your hands and arms out in front of you, you want the sleeves to end at your wrists, where they can either cover the ends of your gloves or vice-versa. In addition, the back of the jacket should extend about three or four inches below your belt line, and should be loose between your shoulder blades. That way, when you're in a riding position on the bike, the back of the jacket won't ride up and expose your lower back, and the material across your upper back won't be stretched tight, making it difficult for you to move your arms. The better-designed riding jackets will have gussets on the shoulder blades, so the jacket can expand across your back when you put your arms out in front of you and fold back together when you're off the bike. Always remember this: a jacket that looks like a perfect fit when you're standing in front of a mirror is probably a very poor choice as a riding jacket. What you really need to do is see how it fits when you're sitting on the bike, with your hands on the handlebars and your feet on the pegs. Then, try leaning from one side to the other, turning your head side to side and turning the handlebars to full lock in both directions. If the jacket doesn't bind or restrict your movements anywhere during this procedure, it's probably a pretty good fit.

Additionally, try to avoid jackets that have anything anywhere on them that's free to flap around in the wind. Here again we see the difference between actual riding jackets and fashion jackets. You might think you would look really cool in one of those leather jackets with the big, floppy collars and loads of fringe down the arms and around the back and shoulders, but in truth, at highway speeds, that fringe will beat you like a hundred little leather whips, while those collars slap you unmercifully on the sides of your helmet. All in all, a really stupid idea, and an easy way to tell the difference between an actual rider and a poser.

Many textile and leather jackets feature perforated material that provides ventilation as well as crash protection.

Pockets

I believe a motorcycle jacket can't have too many pockets, but there are certain criteria that those pockets must meet to be useful. Here again we're talking mostly about the difference between fashion clothing and riding gear.

First of all, all exterior pockets need to have some kind of closure system. Snaps and Velcro fasteners are okay, but you'll be better off with quality, heavy-duty YKK zippers. If possible, try to make sure the zipper pulls are large enough for you to grip and operate with your gloves on. If not, you'll need to add some kind of snap ring or keychain-type attachment to avoid the frustration of having to remove your gloves every time you want something in a pocket. A minor thing, perhaps, but very frustrating.

Secondly, at least one of the pockets needs to be weatherproof, whether on the exterior or inside the jacket. I prefer at least one of each, but you need to have at least one, for keeping things that could be ruined if they got wet.

Left: An exposed metal zipper is a big mistake on a riding jacket. Air and water will pass right through it, the metal itself will get hot and cold according to the weather, and air pressure will push it against your chest.

Center: The only time an exposed metal zipper is at all acceptable is when the jacket is designed with an overlap underneath it, like this. Notice also that though this jacket gives the appearance of a classic old biker style, the collars secure with snaps to keep them from flapping around and the zipper pulls have tabs on them for operating with gloved hands. If you insist on the "cool" look, this is at least an acceptable compromise.

Right: On a modern riding jacket, the minimal acceptable standard should be a single, inside flap protecting you from the zipper. A good touring jacket, however, will have a double-overlap, usually one on the inside and another on the outside, both with closures to secure them in place.

Two side pockets, two breast pockets, and one interior pocket would be the absolute minimum requirement, but a good riding jacket will usually add one or more pockets on the sleeves of the forearms (for easy access to things like change for toll booths), and a larger, pouch-style pocket on the back (for storing a rainsuit or liner).

Basic Construction

By this I simply mean the way the jacket is put together. Though it's a bit difficult to determine for yourself how well constructed a jacket is by just its appearance, there are a couple of clues you can look for. For example, is the thread used to sew the jacket together made from cotton, or is it nylon or Kevlar thread? Is it double-stitched at the critical seams, such as where the arms are sewn onto the shoulders?

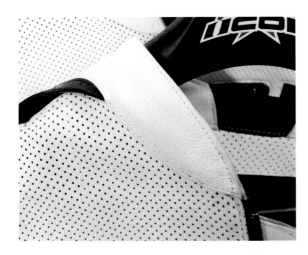

A low, minimalist leather collar like this is only acceptable if, as shown in the lower left photo, it's been lined on the inside with a suede or microfiber material, to avoid chafing. Note the close-up in the lower right photo of the ribbed and unlined leather collar. Can you imagine what your neck would feel like after several hours of head turns, with your sweaty neck rubbing against this?

Are the separate pieces simply sewn at the ends, or is the material overlapped? A quality riding jacket will use nylon or Kevlar thread, double-stitched, with a single or double overlap on the material and a seam-sealing strip of material on the inner side. By its very nature, stitching pokes holes in the material, and those holes need to be covered up. Remember also, if those seams let go while you're sliding down the pavement, all the abrasion-resistant material and body armor in those sleeves isn't going to do you one bit of good. That's why you need the double-stitching and overlapping, with a quality, heavy thread.

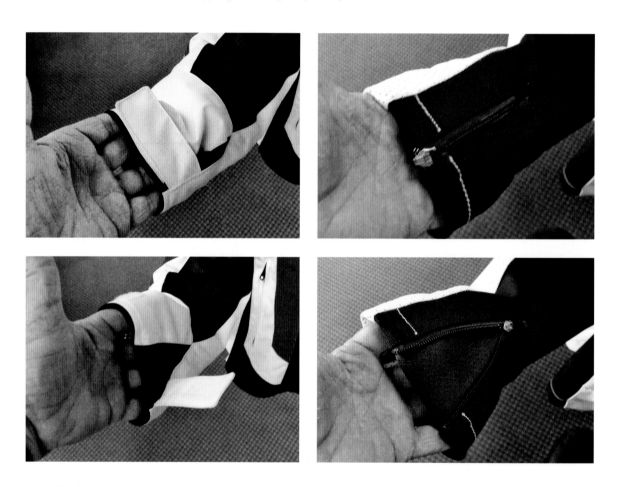

Cuffs should be adjustable, with Velcro, zippers, or snaps, so they can be secured tightly around your wrists or gloves. The closure should also have an inset flap, as both of these do. I prefer zipper closures because I don't trust Velcro not to wear out and come loose. The truth is, however, that Velcro closures are more versatile because they can adjusted to any size you need, while the zippers really can't.

Collar

I suppose most people would hardly think about the collar when looking at a new jacket, but trust me, it's important. First of all, no matter what style or shape the collar takes, make sure the part that actually touches your neck is lined with a soft material. Most good motorcycle jackets will have a special lining around this area, made from suede or microfiber. Remember, when riding we tend to swivel our heads around a lot (if we're doing it right), and the last thing you need is to rub the skin on your neck raw. It's not only a painful distraction, but it will cause you to neglect making those all-important head checks, which could ultimately be fatal.

Collars come in a variety of sizes and shapes; you'll have to decide for yourself which is best for you. Most sport-riding jackets have very narrow, low collars, to allow for maximum

Though it's a bit difficult to determine for yourself how well constructed a jacket is by just its appearance, there are a couple of clues you can look for.

head movement with minimum obstruction. A good touring jacket, on the other hand, might have a larger, fold-down collar that can be flipped up to protect your neck during inclement weather. Some of these even fit nicely under your helmet, to seal you off almost completely in rainstorms, dust storms, or whatever. The main thing to be careful of with these kinds of collars is that they have some kind of retention system to keep them secured when not in use. This is another argument for avoiding fashion jackets, which might have large collars that look great, but which will flap around in the wind and beat against the side of your helmet or your neck.

Cuffs

First of all, your cuffs, like the collars we just discussed, should have a soft lining around the wrist area. If you're riding in a short-sleeved shirt, the cuffs will be rubbing against your wrists every time you clutch, brake, or use the throttle, and your skin will quickly become irritated. Secondly, it's of paramount importance that the cuffs of your riding jacket be adjustable, whether with Velcro, zippers, snaps, or whatever. Sometimes you'll want them fit snuggly under your gloves, while in other situations you may want them to secure over the top of a gauntlet. But whatever the case, you certainly don't want them acting like miniature air scoops, unless it's a particularly hot day. The better jackets will usually have both a zipper and strap of some kind on the cuffs, not only for the reasons we just discussed, but to make the jacket easier to get in and out of.

Closures

Like many of the other features we've talked about, the closures on a riding jacket are both different and much more important than those found on normal, fashion-wear jackets. For example, a simple, exposed zipper down the front is quite common and serviceable on a regular jacket, but a disaster on riding gear. Zippers are not the least bit waterproof or windproof, not to mention that they get really cold when exposed to wind and really hot when exposed to the sun. And believe me, with the air pressure pushing them hard against your chest, you're going to notice those hot/cold/wet pressure points. Still, a zipper is one of the easiest to use and most secure closures you can get, and is found on most riding jackets. The difference with good riding gear is that the primary closure (the zipper) is covered by a secondary closure. This will usually take the form of a single or double overlap, secured by snaps or Velcro. Sometimes the overlap won't have any securing closure, but I would recommend avoiding these. They do a marginal job of keeping the wind and

The sleeves of your jacket should be equipped with some kind of adjusting mechanism, commonly known as "gaiters," so that the jacket and its armor will fit snugly against your arms. The armor, or the simple abrasion protection of the jacket itself, isn't going to do you much good on a get-off if it slides out of place.

rain out of your zipper, but really aren't much good over the long haul, or in severe weather.

All of this also applies, for the most part, to the closures for your pockets, cuffs, and collars, though the overlap is not nearly as critical on the cuffs, due to the fact that these closures are not presented directly in the face of the wind.

Liners

Most decent riding jackets will come with a liner (or even two) that can be removed when you don't need it. Unless you intend on constantly riding in a relatively cold climate, I wouldn't suggest buying any riding jacket with a permanently attached inner liner. Versatility is always the key element.

Primarily you want a liner that will keep you warm, so look for one that's quilted, with a quality insulating material sewn into it. If you're buying a jacket that's made of a mesh material, or is otherwise breathable, then your liner should probably be both wind and waterproof. Unfortunately, many jacket manufacturers will not specify what kind of insulating material is used in their liners, making it difficult for the buyer to judge what he's getting. However, if you can find a label or otherwise determine what kind of insulation is being used, here are a few tips.

If the jacket isn't already designed with ample material across the back for freedom of movement, then it should be equipped with expansion folds, like this. Always check the jacket for full, unrestricted movement with your arms, as if you're going from a lock-to-lock turn.

The waist of your jacket should also be adjustable, and not just with elastic. Look for some kind of strap or belt system, so the waist can be tightened or loosened depending on what you're wearing under the jacket at the time.

These Fieldsheer and Tourmaster jackets exemplify state-of-the-art in motorcycle touring jackets. Note the use of high-visibility colors and reflective piping, double-overlapped closures, venting, zippers with large pulls, inside waterproof pockets that are easily accessible, lined collars, full body armor, zip-out liners, arm gaiters, and adjustable waistbands. For the most part, staying with one of the major manufacturers of modern riding gear will pretty much ensure that you're getting a jacket truly designed for touring.

Originally, the best insulating material you could find was goose down, but that has long since been supplanted by man-made materials that don't pack down or separate as easily. The best-known of these for motorcycle apparel is probably Thinsulate, which outperforms down as an insulator by two to one. However, what the manufacturers aren't too quick to tell you is that Thinsulate can lose up to 20 percent of its insulating properties each time it's washed. The good news is that recent advances have improved on the original formula, producing two newer brand names in insulation: Thermolite and Thermoloft. These will only be found in the more expensive jackets or liners, but insulate up two to three times better than the original Thinsulate, and only lose about 1 or 2 percent of their insulating properties when washed.

Most of the liners that come as part of a riding jacket set are fairly good, but personally, I almost never rely on them. Like many touring riders, over the years I've found aftermarket liners that are more versatile, meet my needs better, and can be used in conjunction with any number of different riding jackets. My two favorites are a quilted, electrically heated liner from Gerbing, and an inflatable, waterproof liner called the AirVantage, by the Gore-Tex company. If the tour I'm leaving on looks like it will probably entail riding through some fairly extreme climate changes, then I'll carry my electric liner. Such was the case when I rode through the Alps, encountering everything from temperatures in the 80s in the German lowlands, to well below freezing in the high Alpine passes of Switzerland. An electric liner, with an attached thermostatic control unit, allows you to simply dial up any amount of heat you need. On the downside, it means attaching an electric pigtail to the bike's electrical system, having to plug in every time you get on the bike, and

THE CE-MARKING PLACED ON THIS PRODUCT CERTIFIES THAT THE PROTECTOR HAS BEEN SUBMITTED THE REQUIREMENTS OF THE EUROPEAN DIRECTIVE 89/686/EEC AND THE TECHNICAL STANDARD 1621-1.

THE PROTECTORS HAVE BEEN DEVELOPED UNDER CONSIDERATION OF THE EEC REGULATIONS AND ESPECIALLY UNDER THE ASPECT OF IMPACT PROTECTION.

If the jacket is equipped with armor (and it really should be), check for a CE marking attesting that it's passed the European Standard. This is the best standard known to date for motorcycling body armor.

especially remembering to unplug before you get off. In addition, as soon as you get off the bike, all of your heating goes away instantly. The AirVantage inflatable, on the other hand, doesn't need any electrical connections or thermostat. Insulation is controlled through the best insulating material in the world—air. The vest is made from a series of sewn-in bladders that you can inflate to varying degrees by simply blowing into a tube near the neck. The more air you blow into it, the better it insulates you. Then, when it gets warmer, you can reverse the cap on the tube and release as much or as little of the air as you need. The AirVantage works quite well, but to a lesser degree than the electric, so it's good for a tour where the temperature fluctuations aren't quite so extreme—say from about 70 degrees down to about 40 degrees. But it also has the advantage of being a very useful garment even after you get off the bike.

BMW sells textile riding suits that are as well-engineered as the company's motorcycles. They are also as expensive as the company's bikes.

Leather vs. Textile

For nearly 30 years now, motorcyclists have argued over the advantages and disadvantages of leather riding gear as opposed to textile. At one time, there really wasn't any contest, as leather outperformed the textiles by a pretty wide margin in almost all categories. Today however, the delineation isn't nearly so clear. With advances in the quality and construction of various nylons and such, higher-end textile jackets can now boast many qualities not only as good as, but in some cases superior to, their leather counterparts, while at the same time there has been a proliferation of lower-end leather riding gear that really doesn't make the grade. So it's not such a clear-cut decision anymore, by any means. A well-made nylon jacket will often be superior to a less-expensive leather one, and conversely, a high-end leather jacket will almost always be superior to a lower-end nylon jacket. Whether you decide on leather or textiles isn't really the question anymore. Instead, you need to know the difference between various grades of leather jackets, and between various grades of textile jackets. We will start with leather.

Leather Motorcycle Jackets

When looking for a leather motorcycle jacket, make sure that the color and texture of the leather is consistent throughout the garment. For example, the leather on the torso and the sleeves of the jacket should look like it came from the same beast. Cheap, knock-off products will be pieced together from scraps left over or discarded from making quality leather goods, and will often be found at swap meets and such, selling for very low prices. Don't be fooled.

Good, quality leather products always begin with the leather itself. Your highest quality products will be made from large pieces of leather that have been graded for blemishes, thickness, and uniformity of grain. Virtually all leather has blemishes. The severity and amount of blemishes determine what type of product it will be used for and for what price. Most deer and elk hides are called "naked leather" and are not treated with any sealant product, which smoothes out and masks blemishes. This is why the products made with naked leather are so much

Two-piece textile riding suits have come a long way in the past few years. They are stylish and functional, and they provide a level of protection equal to almost any leather suit (short of competition-grade) but with a greater comfort level and much lower price.

more pliable and expensive. "Protected hides" are leathers (mostly cowhide, bull hide, and buffalo hide) that have combined the best aspects of natural leather while utilizing tannery technology to create a product that's more uniform in appearance. These leathers are also sealed so that water and other liquids are less likely to stain them, so products made with protected hides are easier to clean and maintain. Most motorcycle jackets are made of this type of leather.

Whether you're buying a jacket made from elk, deer, buffalo, or cowhide, you need to know what kind of quality you're buying. Unfortunately, the grading system used for this purpose is very misleading.

Top-Grain Leather

The most confusing term used in the industry is "top grain." It's a total contradiction in terms, because it implies exactly what it's not. "Top grain" is

Two-piece leather touring suits are still considered the ultimate by many riders, and there are plenty of arguments pro and con between them and the newer textile suits.

the term that's used when the grain is not genuine! This is when the real grain was sanded away to remove or hide imperfections, and an imitation grain was stamped into the leather. When the genuine grain remains, the leather is called "full grain" or "full top grain," not simply "top grain," which is actually an inferior product. Again, don't be fooled.

Full Grain Leather

Just as the grain, texture, and markings of wood should reveal the nature of the tree from which it came, leather should display the natural markings and grain characteristics of the animal from which it was taken. The best leathers are clear, clean, and supple. They're also dyed through with transparent aniline dyes. The full, natural grain is retained, and thus they're called "full grain leather."

Weight

To sum up, cheaper leather has the natural or genuine grain sanded away and an imitation grain pressed or embossed into the surface. It's stiff and has a heavy coating of pigmentation to cover up imperfections. Often, it will look and feel much like plastic.

The better the quality of hide or skin, the less it has to be treated. The natural grain variations should be exposed. One should see the fat wrinkles, and the feel should be supple and natural to the touch.

Finally, the weight of leather used in motorcycle jackets is important and relates to thickness, durability, and protection. A heavier weight means thicker leather and increased protection. Thicker leather also means you'll pay a little more for the quality. Protection and durability are definitely worth the extra cost. Reputable manufacturers will typically specify their leather thickness in terms of weight. Every ounce of weight is equivalent to 1/64 inch of thickness. The weight of leather used in motorcycle jackets, chaps, vests, gloves, and

You have to admit the leather suits look sexy and mark you as a "really serious rider," but for my money, a quality textile suit is a much better value.

other accessories is determined by the number of ounces that one square foot of material weighs. For example, if a square foot of leather weighs four ounces, it's called 4-ounce leather. Some manufacturers will specify weight by ounces, or thickness by fractions of inches, or by millimeters. It all comes down to the same thing, but sometimes you'll need to be able to figure the conversions, such as the one listed above (1/64-inch = .015 inch = 0.396 mm). Using these conversions, for example, a 5-ounce leather jacket has a thickness of .078 in. or 1.98 mm. The reason you need to know this is because of what we talked about before—there are an awful lot of manufacturers out there passing off fashion-weight leather jackets as motorcycle jackets, when they're totally inadequate. A typical rule of thumb for leather would be the following:

0.5 – 0.8mm = Lightweight
0.9 – 1.1mm = Middleweight
1.2 – 1.6mm = Heavyweight
1.7 – 2.0mm = Super Heavyweight

Lightweight leather is good for fashion wear, but should never be used for any kind of motorcycle gear. The protective qualities of this kind of leather are no better than wearing a cotton or denim jacket. Middleweight is generally considered sufficient for items like leather riding pants or chaps, but only marginally acceptable for jackets. Heavyweight is the norm for a good riding jacket, providing a high level of abrasion and impact resistance while still allowing a good range

Lightweight leather is good for fashion wear, but should never be used for any kind of motorcycle gear.

of motion. Super heavyweight is generally reserved for the construction of professional racing suits. This is the highest level of protection you can buy, but it's also very expensive, and not really the kind of gear you would want to wear for long hours of touring day after day.

Textile Motorcycle Jackets

These days, a myriad of synthetic materials are used in constructing motorcycle jackets. Here's a list of the most common, with definitions and some of the terminology associated with them:

Aero-Tex

A thin, lightweight membrane, mounted between the face fabric and the lining. It's waterproof, windproof, and breathable.

Ballistic Nylon

A specific nylon developed by Dupont for the U.S. Department of Defense for use in flak jackets. Later, it was replaced by Kevlar. The basket-weave construction, as opposed to a plain weave, helps add abrasion resistance. The name is used as a marketing tool because "ballistic" makes it sound like something bulletproof, and therefore really tough. Many motorcycle apparel companies use the word "ballistic" when describing material. In many cases the materials' tear and abrasion strength *does not* meet a minimum standard for motorcycle apparel. Basically, the word is used only as a sales gimmick.

Breathability

Humans control body warmth by perspiring and thus prevent their bodies from overheating. When riding, it's necessary to transport at least two pints of perspiration (water vapor) through your clothes every hour. When apparel doesn't breathe, water vapor turns into sweat, and in cold weather, wet heat loss is 23 times greater than dry heat loss. Suits that do not breathe, but use vents, will only be somewhat comfortable in perfect weather. Breathable materials are ideal for motorcycle wear.

CE Armor

"CE" is a European system of grading motorcycle protective armor that encompasses both energy absorption capability as well as pad shape and size. The armor or pads are designed to offer added protection to a rider going down on a motorcycle, particularly in the event of sliding or lesser impacts. CE armor is made of hard foam pieces encapsulated in softer foam, which compresses on impact. If your jacket has body armor in it (and it really should), insist on CE-approved armor.

Cordura

A high-tenacity, air-textured nylon fiber made exclusively by Dupont. Cordura has consistently shown superior abrasion resistance over any other fabric in head-to-head comparisons. Hundreds of nylon materials exist, but 500-denier Cordura is the industry minimum

A one-piece leather riding suit, made from heavyweight or competition-grade leather, is still the very best in protection. However, such suits are usually custom-fitted, very expensive, and not very conducive to long days in the saddle, making them totally impractical for touring riders.

standard for apparel material abrasion and tear strength. (Be cautious when motorcycle clothing manufacturers do not use Cordura in nylon apparel, or use less than 500-denier.)

Denier

A rating for fiber material that provides a scale for the heaviness (largely related to thickness) of fibers in a fabric. The higher the denier, the thicker the fiber. The denier value is defined as the mass in grams per 9,000 meters of yarn. A fiber is generally considered a microfiber if it's one denier or less.

Gore-Tex

Two-piece leather suits can offer nearly the same protection as one-piece suits, provided they can be zipped together.

Like the Aero-Tex listed before, Gore-Tex is a thin, lightweight membrane, mounted between the face fabric and the lining, that's waterproof, windproof, and breathable. Gore-Tex was the original membrane of this type, and totally revolutionized the motorcycle gear materials market with its use in jackets,

suits, pants, gloves, boots, and just about any other piece of riding gear you can imagine. This membrane has nine billion microscopic pores per square inch. These pores are much smaller than a droplet of liquid water, but much larger than a molecule of water vapor. Water in a liquid form cannot penetrate, but both moisture vapor from perspiration and heat can easily escape. The membrane works when the outside temperature is colder than your body temperature, so the membrane actually sucks the heat out of the apparel as long as the outside temperature is lower than 98 degrees Fahrenheit.

Kevlar

The strongest fiber known to man. Kevlar is made by Dupont, and comes in a thread form for apparel use. In a pure weave, Kevlar doesn't stretch and isn't suitable for use in motorcycle apparel, where abrasion is important. In order to give it the proper motorcycle abrasion strength, Kevlar must be woven together with Cordura and Lycra. These are the only suits approved for road racing other than leather. Some gear manufacturers use small portions of pure Kevlar as a gimmick. Quality full suits of it can be found, if you could afford them. This gear is lighter than leather, offers greater protection, and it breathes. It slides on pavement the same way as leather and dissipates friction heat better than leather. Due to its innate toughness during construction and the fabric's limited availability it's not widely marketed, so it will take a bit of looking—and a lot of money—to get one.

Polyurethane

A coating that has a rubber texture and is applied to the inside shell of most nylon. It's used primarily to seal nylon threads when woven into fabric. A lot of nylon motorcycle apparel is 100 percent polyurethane coated and doesn't breathe properly. It's also very important to note that *polyurethane can overheat and melt into your skin during abrasion.* Polyurethane can also trap water after a rain for hours. Even the most expensive apparel can have 20 percent or more polyurethane coating. If you're looking for greater performance and versatility, avoid apparel that has more than a 20 percent polyurethane coating.

PVC (Polyvinyl Chloride)

Nylon alone is not waterproof. In rainsuit and waterproof garment descriptions you'll notice the acronym PVC. This is a rubberized coating that's laminated to the nylon to make it waterproof.

Seam Sealed

When garments are sewn together, the needle creates holes that allow water to pass through. Seam sealing tape is applied to the inside of a stitched seam, using heat to bond the tape to the material, making the seam waterproof. Seam sealing also protects the seam thread from abrasion and premature wear. Any quality motorcycle garment will utilize seam-sealing techniques. Look for it.

Taffeta

A strong, lightweight, breathable nylon that's used primarily for suit linings. Taffeta linings offer the wearer a greater level of comfort because they don't bind against your other clothing, allowing the suit to be put on and taken off with greater ease.

Taslan

Another Dupont invention, Taslan is a means of bulking the fiber to give it better abrasion resistance. Though not often found (yet) in motorcycle gear, if you discover it's used in the jacket you're looking at, consider it a nice plus.

Tri-Armor

Armor comprised of a plastic membrane sandwiched between dual-density, closed-cell, memory armor. Tri-Armor was developed from the results of a four-year crash study in Germany. The goal of this study was to develop the most protective motorcycle suit. Construction and placement of the Tri-Armor was designed to provide the best impact and abrasion resistance. Tri-Armor exceeds the current CE standards.

Ultra Cordura 1000 Denier

The strongest nylon material ever used in a motorcycle suit. It has greater abrasion and tear strength than 1050 Ballistic Cordura. Made by Dupont, this is the first nylon material used in motorcycle apparel made without a polyurethane coating.

Putting It All Together

Even though I tried to keep the items and explanations to a minimum, I probably have you pretty well confused by now. You may be wondering, "How the heck do I choose a good textile riding jacket or suit?" The best I can tell you is to look for a reputable manufacturer that uses a practical combination of the above items. A good example would be a jacket with an outer shell of at least 500-denier Cordura, with a 20 percent or less polyurethane coating, a Gore-Tex or Aero-Tex membrane, a taffeta lining, and CE-approved armor. All that, plus most of the features we described in the general guidelines for construction, fit, collar, cuffs, pockets, closures, and so on. An ideal example would be something like the riding suits produced by the Aerostich company, which was one of the first motorcycle riding gear manufacturers to put it all together in their ground-breaking Roadcrafter suits.

Sunglasses

You might think that there's very little to consider when buying a pair of sunglasses to wear while riding, but you would be wrong. Quite a few things need to be carefully considered when selecting the glasses you intend to ride with.

First of all, remember that sunglasses aren't just fashion accessories. They're a necessary protection for the eyes. Most people know about the danger of sun exposure to the skin, but many are unaware that the sun's rays can damage eyes. To correctly shield your eyes, you must wear the right type of sunglasses, especially since wearing the wrong type can cause more damage than not wearing glasses at all.

The eyes are susceptible to being burned by the sun's rays. The cornea, lens, and retina are all vulnerable to overexposure to ultraviolet (UV) rays. Over time these UV rays—invisible to the human eye—can harm the eye if left unprotected. Long-term exposure to UV rays can lead to cataracts, macular degeneration, or skin cancer around the eyelids. Sunglasses should always be worn when you're riding in the daylight.

It's important to look for the clear substance in sunglasses that blocks harmful UV light. Tinted glasses without UV protection cause more harm than wearing no glasses at all. But you can protect your eyes by simply wearing sunglasses that block out 99 to 100 percent of UV rays. Such glasses protect the eye from both UV-A and the more harmful UV-B rays. Studies show that exposure to ultraviolet light can contribute to a number of ocular complications, including: photokeratitis or snow blindness; cataracts; pterygium (an abnormal growth on the eye's surface); macular degeneration; and even cancer. Tinted contact lens do not protect against harmful rays.

When buying sunglasses, look for a label that says how much UV radiation the lenses of the sunglasses reflect.

When buying sunglasses, look for a label that says how much UV radiation the lenses of the sunglasses reflect. Experts say that sunglasses should block 99–100 percent of both UV-A and UV-B rays. They need to cover the entire eye area, including eyelids.

For riding, you really should buy safety glasses. While conventional sunglasses may protect the eyes from glare, they do a poor job of protecting eyes from flying objects, such as dust, rocks, and insects. In fact, conventional sunglasses can present their own hazards when riding. The frames and lenses used in safety sunglasses are stronger than the frames and lenses used in conventional sunglasses. When an object strikes the lens of the safety sunglasses it's very unlikely that the lens would dislodge. This is not true of conventional eyewear, especially those types with wire frames. When an object strikes the lens of conventional sunglasses, the lens can shatter, showering the wearer's eye with shards of glass or plastic. With a pair of approved safety sunglasses, the lens may break, but it will not shatter back into the eye.

Safety sunglasses can also have shields to reduce the risk of foreign objects reaching the eye from the sides, top, or bottom. Regular sunglasses do not. Because regular sunglasses have a darkened lens, some people mistakenly believe these glasses will provide the needed protection from infrared and UV radiation, but this is not true. Wearing glasses with darkened lenses that are not made to safety glasses specs can actually be more dangerous than wearing no glasses at all. This is because the eye attempts to compensate for less light by opening the pupil wider. In turn, this allows more of the damaging radiation in.

One final note of caution involves polarized lenses, as discussed earlier in this book. If you've forgotten the possible consequences of riding a motorcycle wearing polarized lenses, you might want to look back at that section.

Riding Boots

I think it's safe to say that the most overlooked item of riding gear is proper footwear. I couldn't tell you how many times I've seen riders wearing a decent jacket, helmet, and gloves, but with tennis shoes on their feet. And while it might be true that in higher-speed or more critical accidents, the primary impact points are your head, hands, and arms, it's just as true that in lower-speed,

The following are tips for purchasing safety sunglasses:

Check for the Z87.1 (safety glass) designation

Glasses should be lightweight and adjustable

Label should indicate 99 or 100 percent UV protection

Look for sunglasses that are close-fitting to prevent UV rays from filtering in

Look for larger lenses or wraparound sunglasses to prevent light or other harmful substances from entering the eye

Don't be misguided by price—higher-priced safety sunglasses usually reflect fashion, not level of protection

Know that dark-colored sunglasses don't necessarily provide better protection, because the chemical coating applied to the lens responsible for UV protection is clear

Don't buy those glasses until you've tried them on while wearing your helmet.

If the frames are too wide or tall, or the earpieces don't fit properly through your helmet padding, they're going to be uncomfortable at best, and possibly downright painful.

less-critical accidents (which are considerably more common), it's your feet and ankles that will often bear the brunt of impact. That's probably why, if you go to any large gathering of motorcyclists, you're apt to see a fair percentage of the participants either limping or hobbling around on crutches.

It's also true that much like what we discussed with riding jackets, all too often riders can be found in fashion boots that really aren't designed for motorcycling. Riding boots are designed for very specific purposes, and thinking that any work boot or hiking boot will suffice is a big mistake.

Like almost any other kind of riding gear, boots come in many styles, but as the main focus of this book is on touring, we will stick pretty much to footwear designed for that purpose, and not really get into motocross, off-road, or racing boots, which are considerably different. To this end, we will consider five separate factors: height, soles, materials, construction, and closures.

Height

Motorcycle boots come in various heights, usually from 6-inches to 17-inches tall. The Motorcycle Safety Foundation minimum standard is called "over the ankle," meaning at least 6-inches tall. As the ankle will virtually always become the fulcrum point of stress in a low-speed incident, you really shouldn't wear any kind of footwear that doesn't both cover and support your ankles. Of course, the taller the boot, the heavier it's going to be, and the less comfortable for walking around when off the bike. Generally, the best compromise is to get a boot that's around 10-inches to 12-inches tall. This design will give you a fair amount of ankle support and protection, protect your lower calves from flying debris kicked up by your front tire, insulate you from engine and exhaust heat, and still be moderately comfortable for walking.

Different lens tints filter different wavelengths of light. Some may enhance or distort colors and affect contrast. Here is a basic list of how different tints work, from the Mayo Clinic:

Green
allows true color perception and good contrast in bright light; reduces eyestrain in bright light

Gray
allows true color perception, but does not enhance contrast; good for cycling or running

Brown
good in hazy sun, enhances contrast; good for high-glare environments.

Amber
Brightens cloudy, hazy, or foggy skies; excellent for contrast; minimizes eyestrain; distorts color (images look yellow-orange)

Yellow
improves contrast and depth perception in low light; good for overcast days

Red
excellent depth perception in low light; contrast objects against blue or green backgrounds

Soles

The soles of your riding boots should be oil-, chemical-, slip-, and abrasion-resistant, and a minimum of a half-inch thick. They should also have a tread pattern on them, much like a tire. The most common and best-regarded of these carry the registered trademark Vibram, from a company in Italy known for their durable safety soles, but there are others that are nearly as good. Whatever you do, avoid hard, slick soles such as those found on fashion boots. When you're stopping or starting on an uneven, wet, or oil-slicked surface, the last thing you want is for your foot to slip out from under you. Once 500 pounds of motorcycle starts to fall over, odds are you aren't going to be able to stop it.

Though I know that welted soles like those shown on the previous two pages are more durable over the long haul, I personally prefer cemented ones because of the comfort factor.

Materials

In addition to the Vibram sole material we just talked about, it's important to consider the quality of material used in the construction of the boot itself. First

A well-built pair of motorcycle boots can last you a lifetime.

of all, leather is the most frequent and obvious choice, but just as we discussed in the section about leather jackets earlier, you need to make sure that full grain leather is used, and that it is heavyweight, or at least 1.5mm thick. In addition it should, at minimum, be treated to be water-resistant, but the best situation is when the boot is lined with a breathable, waterproof membrane like Gore-Tex, again just as with the jacket materials we discussed.

Construction

Motorcycle boots should have a minimum number of seams, but even those should be either on the sides, or even better, on the back of the boot, so as not to be exposed to the elements and flying debris. The most important seam, though, is the one that attaches the boot upper to the sole. Basically, soles are attached in one of two ways—welted or cemented. Welting simply means that the sole is stitched to the upper, but with a reinforcing strip of leather or other material sewn in-between. Welting makes a boot stiffer, more stable, and more durable, but also means that the boot won't feel very comfortable when you

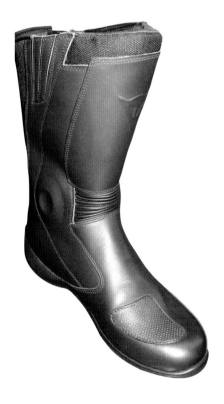
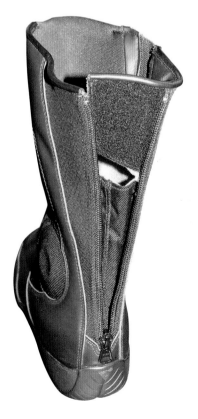

Note that these boots incorporate all of the other best features of a good touring boot: rear closure, tall calf protection, armored ankles, reflective rear piping, shift pad, elastic expanders at the calf and ankle, and thick, slip-resistant soles.

first try walking around in it. Welted boots require a period of break-in before they begin to flex properly with your foot and ankle. Cemented construction is considerably more flexible and will feel comfortable right out of the box, but is not nearly as durable as welting.

It's important to emphasize here once again that you should only consider boots specifically designed for motorcycling. Fashion boots are obviously out of the question, but even heavy-duty work boots are simply not a good idea, since they're designed for an entirely different purpose. Tests by several European safety agencies have shown that work boots made for construction workers and such, while designed to protect the foot from impacts, practically disintegrated when subjected to the kind of high-speed G-forces and abrasion that would be encountered in a motorcycle get-off at speed. This is at least partly due to the type of thread used in the welting process, which in the case of a good motorcycle boot will be much heavier and made from nylon or Kevlar, as opposed to cotton.

In addition to the items just mentioned, which I would consider mandatory in the choice of a riding boot, there are some additional, optional construction features you might want to consider. Among these would be steel-reinforced toes and/or arches, armored ankle protectors, heel reflectors, and a reinforced shifter pad on top of the left toe. None of these are essential, but they're usually the mark of a well-made motorcycle boot.

Closures

Generally speaking, a standard lace-up front closure such as is found on most work boots is not at all a good idea on a motorcycle boot, for a number of reasons. First of all, you don't want anything anywhere on your boots that can come loose, fly free, or get snagged on something at a critical time. Laces expose you to all of these risks, unless they have some kind of secondary closure like a secured flap covering them. And while it's true that laces offer you the versatility of being able to adjust the fit and tightness of your boot, such as when wearing heavier, insulated socks, it's also true that laces are more prone to loosening while riding. So in general, I would advise avoiding lace-up closures for your riding boots. As with the jacket closures we discussed, good, strong YKK-style zippers are usually your best bet. These should be on the outer sides of the boots, with a gusset of waterproof material separating them from the interior and a secondary, secured cover to go over them after they're closed. Remember, the flap of the cover should always close to the rear, whether it secures with snaps, Velcro, or straps.

Of course, you can avoid the problem of closures entirely with pull-on boots, but personally I've never found any that fit as snugly as I would like, even when equipped with built-in elastic expanders. And quite frankly, the elastic stretches out over time, making the boots fit a little bit worse every time I put them on.

Riding Gloves

Most touring riders will own at least two or three pair of riding gloves for varying weather conditions. I travel with a lightweight, vented pair for hot-weather riding in the desert, a standard touring set, and a pair of heavyweight, insulated, and waterproof gauntlets for foul weather.

My lightweights have soft leather palms, with reinforcing skid pads, but the backs are made from a nylon mesh, with articulated armor panels on the knuckles. They have short wrists (gauntlets) and adjustable Velcro closures. My standard gloves are made from deerskin, with padded palms and a thin layer of insulation on the backs. They have slightly longer wrists, but don't have any real armor. My heavyweights are 100 percent textile, made from Cordura nylon with Gore-Tex linings, and have large gauntlets with double-securing straps for going over my jacket cuffs.

In general, follow the guidelines given for riding jacket materials when buying your gloves. Most of the same advice applies. Seams should be double-stitched with heavy nylon or Kevlar thread, with one important caveat: all the stitching should be on the *outside* of the glove. Interior stitching, often found on cheaper gloves, will rub painfully against your fingers and thumbs while operating the controls. In addition, well-designed riding gloves will always be pre-curved, that is, designed and sewn together in such a way that

Gloves are critical pieces of safety gear for a number of reasons, but primarily because it's basic human nature in an impending accident situation to throw our hands out in front of ourselves for protection.

even without your hands in them, they will naturally take the shape of a hand loosely gripping a throttle. If not, after several hours of riding you'll develop fatigue and cramps in your hands from forcing the fingers to curve into a grip.

Gloves are critical pieces of safety gear for a number of reasons, but primarily because it's basic human nature in an impending accident situation to throw our hands out in front of ourselves for protection. Among professional motorcycle racers, hand injuries are by far the most common for this very reason. Because of this, you really should wear gloves that incorporate at least some level of armor.

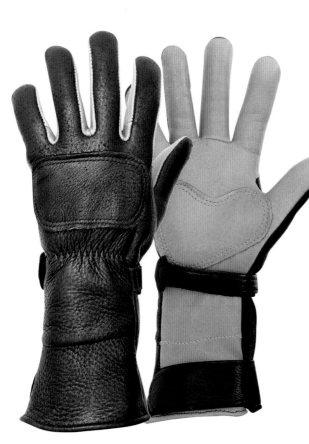

Deerskin gauntlets like these from Lee Parks Design (left) are among my favorite standard touring gloves. The deerskin is supple, strong, and comfortable, with a layer of insulation on the back to protect from the wind but no insulation on the palm side, which provides better control feel and allows the use of heated handgrips. The only drawback is a lack of serious armor, though you will note some decent extra abrasion pads on the palms and on the knuckle areas.

My rain gauntlets (below) have three separate securing methods for keeping them tight and sealed on my hands, plus some reflective piping for extra visibility in bad weather, and a rubberized coating on the palms to keep them from slipping on the controls when wet.

Note that these gloves have a special built-in wiper for clearing your faceshield. If you ride much in the rain, a feature like this will really come in handy.

Granted, on my hot-weather gloves that's confined to nothing more substantial than some light polystyrene panels on the knuckles and a reinforcing pad on the palms, but this should be the absolute minimum you settle for. However, even if you get strong Kevlar armor on the knuckles and backs of the fingers, make sure that the armor is articulated—that is, that it's sectioned so that the glove can bend where it needs to.

Though leather is still the weapon of choice for most motorcycle gloves, more and more we're seeing a combination of leather and textiles in the better touring gloves. Ideally, you would want a pliable, reinforced leather palm (for maximum abrasion resistance) that's still thin enough to give you a good feel for the controls. The backs could be either leather or Cordura, with articulated thermoplastic, titanium, or Kevlar armor covering critical impact points. All stitching should be outside, and doubled. The fingers should be pre-curved and flex easily.

If you're buying foul-weather gloves, it's usually best to stick to basic nylon construction and avoid leather, and as with the materials we talked about for jackets, go for a breathable waterproof liner, such as Gore-Tex. Also make sure the gauntlet fits well over the cuffs of your jacket, and can be snugged down securely.

The left and center photos are my two different types of summer gloves, which I use for riding in the desert when temperatures routinely exceed 100 degrees Fahrenheit. The pair from Cortech, on the left, are heavily vented, with plastic armor and ribbed abrasion pads. These offer the most protection but still get pretty hot. When I just can't take the heat, I switch to the pair from OSI, on the right, which are made from nylon mesh for great ventilation but which offer no real impact or abrasion protection beyond a thick pad on the back of the knuckles. If you want absolutely no protection at all, you could get some of the fashionable "fingerless" gloves shown, but these have no safety value whatsoever.

Another option to consider, and one which I've used at times, is to carry only a single pair of good leather touring gloves with several specialized liners to put under them. There are silk liners for comfort, fleece or Thermolite for warmth, Gore-Tex and other membranes for waterproofing, Hipora for wind protection, and so on. With these, and other types that fit over the glove rather than under, you can adapt your gloves to almost any weather conditions.

Rainsuits

Unless you've made the major investment (usually well over $1,000) in an all-purpose riding suit, you're going to need a rainsuit if you're going to tour. For most of us, carrying a moderately priced rainsuit that packs up small is the best option.

Waterproofing for motorcycle rainsuits comes in four basic forms: waxed cotton, PVC-coated polyester, polyurethane-coated nylon, and breathable microporous membranes.

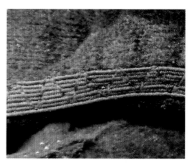

Always look for overlapping material at the seams, with double or even triple stitching. Turn the glove inside out if you have to, to check. If the stitching is inside the glove, it should be covered by a lining or by ribbing (as in the lower photo). You don't want the stitching rubbing against your skin.

Nylon thread—preferably Cordura—is best. Cotton is okay only if it appears in multiple strands of a dozen or more. Don't be fooled by a manufacturer touting Kevlar thread, unless he can show you that the overlap at the seams has been heavily reinforced. Without lots of extra reinforcing of the material, on the stress of impact, the Kevlar thread will not break (that's the obvious selling point) but instead will simply cut through the glove material like a hot knife through butter. In the best case, it will shred your gloves, and in the worst, it will shred your skin, also.

Waxed Cotton

Waxed cotton raingear was originally developed for sailors, and gained great popularity with motorcyclists in the 1950s and 1960s, before man-made textiles became commonly available. Today, it's probably the least-popular alternative, though a lot of purists and old-timers still swear by it. Waxed cotton raingear is very durable and long-lasting, and does a great job of keeping you dry, but it doesn't breathe well and is quite bulky.

PVC-coated

PVC-coated (polyvinyl chloride) polyester or cotton raingear is generally inexpensive and exceptionally waterproof. It's also heavy, bulky, and doesn't breathe at all. Try to imagine one of those sauna suits. In anything less than a cold, driving rain, you'll quickly become very uncomfortable in one of these suits.

Polyurethane-coated

Polyurethane-coated nylon (preferably Cordura, as we spoke of with the riding jackets) is usually more expensive and has better abrasion resistance than the PVC-coated materials we just spoke of, but carries most of the same drawbacks.

Breathable Microporous Membranes

Breathable microporous membranes such as Gore-Tex and Aero-Tex have virtually taken over the world of motorcycling raingear in the past few years, and for good reason. When sandwiched between layers of nylon or polyester, these membranes provide 100 percent waterproofing while still allowing air and water vapors to pass

Perhaps the best alternative to carrying a rainsuit is to purchase an all-weather, all-purpose, armored riding suit, like this one from BMW. The problem is, they cost a ton. I believe this one retailed for over $1,200.

through. That means you stay cool even when buttoned up tight. Such suits are usually comparably priced to the others, while being lighter and taking up less packing space. The main thing to look out for with such suits is how much stitching they have. When these membranes are punctured by needles, you create not only entry points for moisture, but weak points in the membrane that can stretch and tear. If there's any stitching in the suit, look for the least amount possible, and make sure that the seams are double-overlapped and securely sealed from the inside.

Polyvinyl rainsuits are the least expensive and most waterproof riding suits you can buy. Problem is, they don't breathe—at all. Great for riding in a cold, winter rain, but in anything less, you'll sweat like a pig under one of these sauna suits. Right: Most of us will never look this good in our raingear, but there's no harm in trying.

Frogg Toggs

Though I don't want this book to come off as an info-mercial for any single product, I don't believe it would be wrong of me to mention that my personal favorite in raingear for a number of years has been something called Frogg Toggs. These suits come in a variety of styles but all are made from a triple layer of polypropylene with a center layer of microporous film. They use no stitching, with seams that are double-folded and sealed, weigh less than one pound, and can be compressed down to about the size of two softballs. True, they're not nearly as durable as the other types, and will need to be replaced about every third or fourth season, but considering that they cost about half the price of the others, I consider them a bargain.

My favorite rainsuits are the two-piece ones from Frogg Toggs, shown here in their original packaging (right), and stuffed into the carrying pouch that comes with them (left). As you can see, they pack up fairly small and are very light; they do a great job of keeping me dry. They're not terribly durable, though, as I manage to wear out a pair every two or three seasons of riding, but for around $50 a pair, I figure that's a bargain.

Me in an older, more colorful set of Frogg Toggs, braving the "rainiest week in Knoxville, Tennessee, in over 20 years," according to a local TV weatherman.

As with the riding jackets we discussed earlier, there are certain general characteristics you need to look for when shopping for a rainsuit:

There should be as few seams as possible, and if stitched, they should be overlapped, double-stitched, and sealed. If glued or heat-sealed, make sure the contact area is wide and/or overlapped, and sealed on the inside. Generally speaking, this type of seam is preferable on raingear, as it completely eliminates needle holes, which are always potential leak points.

Collars, wrist, and pant cuffs should be adjustable and close snugly and securely. If possible, get a collar that can be raised up around your chin, under the helmet.

All closures should have wide overlaps that close snugly.

Vents should be kept to a minimum or eliminated altogether, as should any entry points for getting to your pockets or fly. Sure, such openings make getting to your interior parts easier and more convenient, but they also make easier entry points for water.

Try to get a suit that can pack as small as possible. With any luck, you aren't going to be wearing it that often.

If the suit is a two-piece, make sure the jacket comes down well below the pant line, especially in the back.

Always buy your rainsuit large enough that you can wear heavy insulated gear underneath it.

If at all possible, buy a rainsuit with retro-reflective strips on the back, arms, and legs. Or, at the very least, be sure to buy your suit in bright colors. Remember, most of the time when wearing it, you're going to be riding in traffic during periods of highly restricted visibility.

Earplugs

If you ride a motorcycle without using hearing protection, you will, in time, become at least partially—if not totally—deaf. At the risk of using a really bad pun, hear me out.

Most of us know that we shouldn't ride motorcycles without wearing earplugs, and yet the majority of us (including me, until recently) still do it on a regular basis. I believe that one of the major contributors to this problem is simple misinformation regarding the causes and ultimate effects of motorcycle-induced hearing loss. I myself believed in a lot of the myths surrounding the subject, until I bothered, at the urging of my old friend and motorcycling guru, David Hough, to really research the subject. At first I intended to just skim through the reams of material I found, but the deeper into the scientific studies I got, the more fascinated I became with just how ignorant I really was on the matter. And so, to hopefully save some of you from having to wade through the same material, I'd like to share the high points of what I learned. Naturally I don't have the space here to list all the resources (31 separate studies), or even briefly touch on all of the methodologies and conclusions, so I'll just have to ask you trust me when I say that the conclusions listed here are all backed by significant and well-researched data and experimentation by hundreds of the best minds in the field, worldwide.

Swedish, Dutch, British, American, and German studies have all experimented with various solutions to this problem, and all reached the same conclusion: the best option would be for someone to design a totally new kind of motorcycle helmet—one with attenuation (sound-reducing quality) of at least 30dB. Problem is, no one has been able to design such a helmet in a size, weight, and impact-absorbing level that would be viable for use by motorcyclists. Which leaves us with the second-best option of simply wearing earplugs every time we ride. According to the studies, the best of these are the custom-molded kind, but the foam disposables come pretty close to being just as good, so long as you make sure they have an attenuation rating of at least 30dB. I've purchased at

> **I myself believed in a lot of the myths surrounding the subject, until I bothered, at the urging of my old friend and motorcycling guru, David Hough, to really research the subject.**

Wind noise is by far the primary culprit in causing hearing loss among motorcyclists. In scientific circles, it's known as "the silent killer," because we tend not to notice it much. Ambient noise from traffic, or our own engines or exhausts, even on very loud bikes, accounts for no more than 3 percent to 5 percent of the damaging noise that reaches our ears.

Wind noise reaching your ears is 10 times greater when not wearing a helmet than when wearing a full-face model.

Despite what item number two says, even when wearing a full-face helmet, you're exposed to noise levels higher than those allowed by OSHA's industrial regulations for someone operating a chainsaw.

Even though a full-face helmet will reduce your exposure to wind noise, it has been found that many models actually resonate as they vibrate from the passage of wind around them, creating low-frequency resonance sound waves that can't really be heard, but which damage your hearing even more severely than the wind noise they're blocking out!

Wind noise increases on a curve relevant to speed, but actually reaches danger levels very quickly, at only 30 mph, and then increases on a linear scale from there all the way up to 100 mph (the highest speed tested). If you think you don't need hearing protection for just riding around town, you're wrong.

Full fairings, windshields, faceshields, and so on do little to reduce damaging wind noise. At best, they only reduce the levels by around 5 percent, and in certain cases, they can actually increase the levels of low-frequency damage. For years, I thought that while riding my Gold Wing, with its extra-quiet engine and giant, full fairing, I really didn't need earplugs. I was wrong.

Riding position and/or the style of bike (cruiser vs. sportbike vs. luxury tourer) has little or no effect on the wind noise levels reaching your ears.

Helmet padding, chin shields, open or closed vents, or even air dams molded into the helmet shell to alter airflow patterns have virtually no effect on reducing wind noise.

Wind noise doesn't just damage your hearing, it has been proven to induce fatigue, loss of equilibrium, and to reduce your concentration level, making your ride both more tiring and more dangerous.

Riding for four hours at 35 mph has been proven to generate enough wind noise to harm your hearing. At 65 mph, only two hours of riding will cause permanent, irreparable damage to your hearing. At 80 mph, it only takes 15 minutes of exposure to create the same amount of damage. Sure, the damage will be slight, and you may not even notice it at the time, but it's cumulative. It never goes away, and each ride adds a little more to the total damage level.

least three sets of custom-molded earplugs, but the truth is that I either neglect to clean them, which has resulted in a nasty ear infection, or I lose them. So I've finally gotten into the habit of buying disposables in packs of 100, and keeping them on the bike and in my riding jacket pockets.

For the first 20 years that I rode, I can at least claim that I was totally ignorant of the need to protect my hearing. Unfortunately, for the second 20 years, I have to take the blame for ignoring both the warning signs and a lot of good advice. Now, if I'm lucky enough to last that long, it seems that for the final 20 years, I'll need to be extremely vigilant in trying to protect what little hearing I have left.

As I sit here in my home office writing this, I have a persistent and annoying ringing in my ears. Someone rang my doorbell about an hour ago, and I didn't hear it. Only my dog barking alerted me to the person's presence. In the evenings, my wife complains because I turn the TV up too loud. It's called tinnitus, and I'm told my case is moderate to severe, and will never get any better. It will, however, get worse every time I take the bike out for another ride. All I can hope to do now is slow down its progress.

Please, please don't end up like me.

Here are a variety of different types of earplugs. Choose the type that works best for you. The important thing is that you wear them.

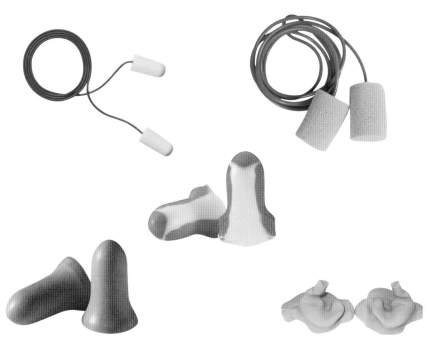

Chapter 7
Bike Accessories

Back in 1990, when Bob Carpenter and I were first mulling over the concept that would eventually become *Motorcycle Consumer News*, one of the items we spoke about and easily agreed upon was the criteria we would use to decide which accessories were worth reporting on, testing, and evaluating. We were both of the same mind: the primary factor would always be functionality. If an item demonstrated, or even claimed to in some manner improve your bike, or your general riding experience, then it was worthy of reporting. On the other hand, those items which were strictly for appearance's sake, or which could not be construed in any way to be helpful to motorcyclist, were summarily discarded. Basically, I'm following that same principle here in this book. And though I obviously can't cover all the types of accessories available for your bike (just take a look at any of those 500-page

There was a time when I was a total accessories junkie, as evidenced by my 1981 Gold Wing. I counted them up once, and if I remember correctly, I purchased and attached 302 aftermarket accessories to this bike. Quite a few of them were electrical, and since the older Wings didn't have the oversized alternators that equip today's Wings, I fried two alternators before finally having the main wiring harness actually catch on fire. Live and learn, I guess.

catalogs selling them!), we will at least discuss the most common types, and a few general guidelines for deciding what might be worth purchasing.

I wish someone had given me some of this advice 40 years ago, as demonstrated by ...

Suspension Mods

There are hundreds, if not thousands, of products you can buy to modify the suspension on your bike, from cartridge emulators to specialized valving, to progressive-rate springs, to pretty much anything else you can imagine and then some. For the most part, they will make a marked improvement in your bike's ride and handling characteristics. I know that personally, I've been astounded at times to ride a recently converted test bike that I previously considered a lumbering ox, only to find that it was a totally different machine after something as simple as getting a new set of fork springs. But it can be just as true that if the new suspension components aren't properly matched to your bike, or even if they just aren't set up properly (one of my personal failings), they might have virtually no effect at all. In the worst-case scenario, which I've also experienced, they can actually make a bike ride rougher and handle worse, to the point of being dangerous. This happens most often in the case of lowering kits, which sacrifice ride height, cornering clearance, and suspension travel for the sake of short-legged riders. And don't even get me started on things like springer-style front suspensions or hardtail choppers.

I know that personally, I've been astounded at times to ride a recently converted test bike that I previously considered a lumbering ox, only to find that it was a totally different machine after something as simple as getting a new set of fork springs.

In most cases, however, if your bike isn't handling properly, the suspension tends to bottom out, top out, or give you any other kind of problem, chances are you don't need to spend a lot of money on new parts—you just need to learn how to adjust your stock suspension properly. As these adjustments vary somewhat by the type and brand of bike, and the detailed explanation of how to accomplish a proper setup can easily run 10 or 12 pages long, rather than try to describe it here, I am going to suggest that you either consult an expert at your local shop, or utilize the Internet. There are dozens of great tutorials now available online, including how-to videos from people like Keith Code on YouTube.

Aftermarket Pipes

While it's true that many aftermarket exhausts can improve both the horsepower output and the gas mileage of your engine, I believe it's just as true that the

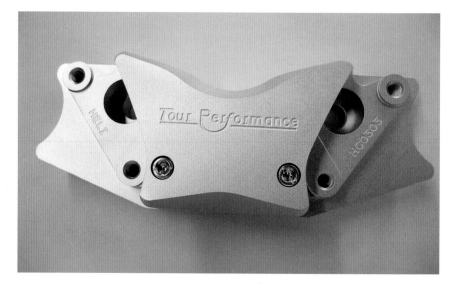

One of the more popular aftermarket items for many bikes is some kind of handlebar relocator. This one from Tour Performance was installed under the handlebars of my Honda ST1300, to bring them three-quarters of an inch closer to me and a half an inch higher. You wouldn't believe how such a small adjustment could improve your comfort on long rides. This is a "fixed" adjustment, but there are other systems—for a lot more money, of course—that are adjustable after they're installed.

majority of add-on pipes actually rob a bike of power, and make it run much worse than it did with the stock setup. Still, most riders buying them couldn't care less. All they want is the sound. The sad part is that if they bought the right kind of pipes, and had their bike's fuel and ignition mapping (or carburetors) set up properly to match the modified backpressure, they could have the best of both worlds. But you and I both know they just buy the loudest pipes they can find, bolt them on in their garage, and ride away, usually with a bike that's now running far too rich a fuel mixture, resulting in engine overheating and carbon buildup. But hey bro, they sound cool, huh?

For the touring rider, in general, aftermarket pipes are a complete waste of money.

Handlebar Relocators

I've used several different kinds of handlebar relocators over the years, and in general believe they're one of the best modifications you can make to your bike. The ergonomic fit between you and your bike can make a world of difference not only in your comfort, but in your control of the bike. Handlebar kits allow us the opportunity to modify the stock positioning to fit our personal needs. The problems usually come about when we really don't know how to set them up. Remember, any change at all in the geometry of your steering setup will affect how it reacts to your inputs, and you have to be especially wary of moving your bars into a position that might cause them to strike your tank in a full-lock turn. And of course, at the extreme end of any discussion like this, I can't help but mention those incredibly stupid ape-hanger bars that have been popularized by TV and the movies. Whoever dreamed those things up ought to be bitch-slapped into the next century.

While most full-bore luxury touring bikes and cruiser touring bikes feature handlebars that are already in what you might call a "relaxed" position, it's just as true that most sport-touring bikes, like the Honda ST, Yamaha FJR, and BMW RT, come from the factory with bars that are in a slightly more forward, or sporting position. These are the bikes that you'll most commonly find have been modified by their owners with relocation devices of one type or another. Such relocators come in forms that vary from fairly simple shimming devices to complex systems that can be adjusted not only forward and back but up and down and in varying degrees of angle.

A word of caution: before buying any kind of relocating device for your bars, make absolutely certain that all of your control cables, wiring, and hydraulic

Continued on page 166

Parable:
The Accessories Junkie

You like to buy accessories for your bike, don't you? Sure you do. You're a motorcyclist, and a motorcyclist's second favorite thing to do, after riding, is usually buying accessories. For **some** of us, it becomes an addictive obsession.

Ever seen the feeding frenzies at the vendor shows at Americade, Daytona, Sturgis, and other major rallies? Piranha would be frightened.

According to several reports on the motorcycle aftermarket, the average new motorcycle buyer purchases around $800 worth of accessories during his first year of ownership, then about $400 per year for the next several years after that. But that's just the **average**.

The truly hard-core accessory buyers, it seems, are two distinctly disparate groups who would normally seem to have little else in common: Harley owners and Gold Wing owners. These two groups are said to average close to $2,000 each in accessory purchases for their bikes the first year, dropping off to around $1,200 per year for the next several years after that. Want to get rich quick? Invent and market the next must-have doodad for big bike owners.

Personally, I divide accessories into two distinct classes: ornamental and functional. On the ornamental front, billet or chromed parts that do absolutely nothing better than the ones they replace except look better, has spawned a billion-dollar

industry. And don't even get me started on lights—especially the new fiber optics and high-intensity LEDs. Conspicuous consumerism, it seems, runs more rampant among our ranks than through almost any other sport in the world. I could probably retire quite nicely on only the profits from engraved "Live to Ride" timing case covers for Harleys, or chromed plastic disc brake covers for GLs.

Even a seasoned tour rider like Brian Rathjen, editor of Backroads *magazine, can fall prey to the allure of multiple accessories. Using the excuse that he needed to test things for the magazine, Brian had so many accessories wired into his beloved BMW GS that the wiring harness caught fire while we were riding through the Adirondacks.*

About 25 years ago, I was one of the worst offenders. My particular obsession involved lights. Besides the stock lighting on my 1983 GL, I had fog lamps (with covers that opened and closed automatically when turned on and off), lower light bars around the saddlebags, an upper light bar around the trunk, a lighted license plate frame, six lighted accessory rocker switches, lighted front disc brake covers, and dual lighted radio antennas. The CB antenna even had a little gizmo called a "firefly" on the tip that lit up whenever I keyed the mike. If I remember correctly, I had 187 extra bulbs wired into the Wing's electrical system. Needless to say, batteries lasted me an average of about 90 days, and the alternator had to be rewired on a fairly regular basis. I comforted myself with the thought that I really wasn't all that bad, because I knew another guy who had over 300 lights on his bike—so many that he'd to carry a spare, full-sized car battery in his saddlebag to keep from frying his charging system. I only wish there had been a 12-step program for guys like us back then—"Hello. My name is Fred, and I'm a lighted accessory junkie."

I eventually kicked my lighting habit, and later a slightly less severe addiction to chrome, but I never have gotten over my unquenchable desire for gadgets. In that sense, I don't believe I'm any different from most of the motorcyclists in America. But at least I can claim that as I've grown older, I've done a much better job of limiting my gadget purchases to those items that are more sensible and practical. I no longer reach reflexively for my wallet when I pass a vendor booth offering a three-speed electric windshield wiper and de-icer system with intermittent timer control. Though I'll admit to having dreams lately about BMW's prototype Bluetooth helmet with heads-up, infinite focus digital instrument display.

As you can see, I now have my addiction under fairly good control. This puts me on a higher plane, and allows me to look down and snicker with great self-satisfaction at those lesser souls who still buy mahogany dashboard bezels and lighted valve stem caps.

However, every June I head to New York to once again attend my favorite motorcycle rally—Americade, home to the largest motorcycle accessories trade show this side of Munich's Intermot. While there, I'll marvel once again at the hordes of zombie-like creatures prowling the TourExpo, each clutching a badly scarred credit card in one hand and a portable two-way radio in the other, which they use to inform their peers the very moment they spot yet another totally unique whatchamacallit for their bike. If the rally organizers had any sympathy for these poor wretches at all, you'd think they would offer counseling sessions, or at the very least post warning signs with phone numbers for self-help centers, like casinos do for compulsive gamblers. It's time we recognized that accessory addiction is an illness, and treated it accordingly.

I pity these poor souls—I really do—as only a reformed compulsive accessory buyer can. Maybe someday they'll mature, like I did, and learn to control their urges. Heck, I exercised so much self-control last year that I've already paid off the balance on my credit card, with a whole month left to go before the next Americade.

And so, let us proceed to accessories.

Continued from page 163

lines have enough slack to reach to the new position without kinking or pulling when you steer to full-lock. If they don't reach easily, either your relocator is going to have to be sold on eBay, or you're going to spend many hundreds of dollars on replumbing your controls.

Auxiliary Lighting

Like many modification accessories, auxiliary lighting can be a real blessing to motorcyclists. Especially since, as we all know, the stock lighting on many bikes is totally inadequate for doing something so foolish as actually riding after dark. Fork, frame, and even fairing-mounted driving lights can go a long way toward lighting up the shoulders of a dark country road while on the lookout for errant deer and other ruminants, or seeing those sneaky potholes that come up out of nowhere. So long as they're mounted and aimed properly, they can really improve your safety. I would say the same about auxiliary brake lights, even those somewhat annoying ones that flash, as long as they get the job done, and the job is conspicuity—getting drivers to notice you. But I think the jury is still out on headlight flashers. I realize they do make you more conspicuous, but I can't help but wonder if they don't also piss off other road users, and perhaps

While stock lighting on motorcycles has improved dramatically over the years, it can always be improved upon.

sometimes even contribute to the phenomenon of target fixation. Whatever the case with any of these, at least they seem to have function, which is more than I can say for things like the popular Ring of Fire that puts red and blue LEDs around the front brake rotor of Gold Wings, or the new fashion of running colored neon lights in your undercarriage. Still, in all, I imagine such things are harmless, so I really can't say anything too bad about extra lighting of any kind on a bike. Like I said, the name of the game is conspicuity and visibility.

Personally, when it comes to auxiliary lighting to enhance my headlights, I'll opt for fork-mounted units, simply because at low speeds they turn with your handlebars, thus throwing more light in the direction you're heading. Fairing- and frame-mounted lights can be good too, but won't turn as quickly into your direction of travel.

Continued on page 172

One of the easier and more practical methods of accessorizing your bike is to replace your stock headlight bulbs with Sylvania's "Silverlight" bulbs, or to go all the way by installing high-intensity discharge (HID) lighting. You can see the obvious difference in this photo, with a PIAA HID next to a stock headlight on this Suzuki SV. The difference in road illumination when riding at night is phenomenal.

Rockin' Down the Highway

Almost 30 years ago, I rigged up my first on-bike audio system so I could listen to music while riding. At first it consisted of nothing more complex than a portable cassette tape player, which I carried in my pocket, and a normal set of earphones stuck in my ears. But it had a lot of drawbacks: the earphones tended to pop out of my ears when I put my helmet on, the batteries in the tape player weren't good for more than about two hours of playtime before they had to be replaced, the tapes themselves only played for 30 minutes before they had to be taken out and flipped over, and the sound volume was barely powerful enough to be heard at low speeds. The setup was completely useless on the highway.

Over the years, though, as technology marched forward, I was able to refine my system bit by bit, until it became at least marginally effective. I'll never forget how thrilled I was when I found my first cassette player that would automatically reverse itself and play both sides of the tape. That was even further enhanced when new, longer-format tapes came out, with 45 minutes to a side. Now I could listen for an entire 90 minutes, if the batteries held out that long. However, I was soon

The introduction of radios to motorcycles was a major advance to music fans like me.

When motorcycle entertainment centers start having video screens, it's an indication that this whole touring amenity thing might be going a bit too far.

to learn the hard way that the longer the tape, the more inclined it was to get snarled up in the mechanism, and also that dragging the weight of all that extra tape over the capstans tended to deplete my batteries even faster than normal.

Then came two fantastic innovations: the alkaline battery, and a little device called the Boostaroo. The new batteries could power my tape player almost twice as long as before, and the Boostaroo pumped up the volume of the unit to where I could actually hear the lyrics to the songs at highway speeds, even in heavy traffic. For those of you who have yet to discover this little marvel, it's nothing more complex than a small, battery-powered amplifier that plugs easily into almost any kind of audio device. Not only does it boost the sound level tremendously, but it saves on battery power for

your main unit and splits the audio signal into two or three output jacks, so both you and your passenger can use it at the same time. I still use a Boostaroo to this day, over a decade later, though now with things like iPods and other mp3 players.

But as good as my new setup was, it couldn't hold a candle to the new, OEM-installed, on-bike audio systems that were beginning to make their presence felt at around this same time. My first was on a Honda GL1100 Interstate, which sported a fairing-mounted AM/FM radio and cassette player, with speakers built right into the bike's fairing. All my friends and neighbors were astounded.

This system, and similar ones on bikes like the Yamaha Venture and Harley Electra Glide, would become the standard for on-bike audio for the next 15 years or more, with very little in the way of innovation or improvement along the way. In fact, I would venture to say that when comparing my 1980 GL's audio system to that on my 2000 GL, I really couldn't find a whole lot of improvement. Twenty years really only brought us slightly better speakers and headsets, a few little tricks like automatic volume control, and the eventual replacement of the cassette tape with the compact disc. Improvements to be sure, but hardly to the degree one would expect for a two-decade timespan.

But then digital music took a big leap, from the compact disc to the mp3 player. My music library, which had shrunk from about 500 cassette tapes to around 80 CDs, could now be housed in its entirety in a little cube roughly the size of a pack of cigarettes. Hundreds and hundreds of hours of tunes, reproduced in a quality so flawless it would have made a 1960s audiophile drool, now reside in my shirt pocket, to be called forth at my slightest whim. I can preset graphic equalizers to get the most out of different kinds of recordings, tap into bass booster circuits for an arena-like concert sound, create surround-sound effects, or do any other of a myriad of things that would have required a room full of expensive equipment only a few years ago. And perhaps my favorite: I can build playlists of various kinds of music, suited for different kinds of riding. In just the past few months I've tapped into Bob Seger and the Silver Bullet Band for spirited background music to a ride through the San Bernardino Mountains, and

The advent of handlebar-mounted radio controls was a major safety advancement because it allowed the rider to adjust the radio without taking his hands off the handlebar.

called on John Denver to keep me company while I meandered through the back roads of Tennessee and North Carolina. And, suddenly realizing that nothing could be more appropriate for the setting, on a recent night ride through the north Georgia mountains, I pulled over for a moment to flip through my audio files and bring up the late, great Ray Charles, singing his incomparable version of "Georgia on My Mind."

I know there are a lot of riders who feel that listening to music has no place on a motorcycle, but I'm of the exact opposite opinion. Sure, if I'm riding hard, pushing the envelope a bit on some piece of particularly challenging road, I don't want or need the distraction of music playing in my ears. But, on the other hand, if I'm just out to enjoy the ride, and the ambience of all the sensory inputs that go into it, then I feel that the right background music only enhances the experience.

In 2006, I was invited along on Honda's press introduction of the newest GL1800 Gold Wing. Though most of the rest of the press contingent took little notice of the fact, I was impressed to note that one of the major improvements to that year's Wing was a whole new audio system. Replacing the standard, four-speaker, 30-watt per channel unit that had been the bike's mainstay for so many years, was an awesome, six-speaker, 80-watt per channel unit, fit to do battle with any stereo system. I swear, if you crank this baby up to full volume while sitting in a parking lot, it will practically make you bleed from your ears, and is guaranteed to rattle windows 50 yards away—and all that without any discernible distortion.

*I know—you're thinking, "Who needs that kind of power?" Well, nobody really. But it sure is nice to have when you're doing 80 mph on the L.A. freeway in heavy traffic. And I have to admit it did my evil little heart a world of good one day, when a lowrider full of homeboys stopped next to me at a traffic light with their hip-hop music pounding out of the car's windows. I just thumbed the volume control on the left handlebar, and completely drowned them out with a recording of Josh Groban singing opera—in Italian. All four heads swiveled my way at once, with a look of shock and dismay that was priceless.

Thanks, Honda.

These days, with the rapidly advancing technology of digital music players, and new headsets and earphones that easily adapt to being used inside a helmet, the possibilities for a rider to listen to music are almost endless. My newest setup includes an mp3 player that holds over 5,000 songs, an AM/FM radio, weather radio, and even XM satellite radio, all transmitted wirelessly to my helmet, which is equipped with a dual-frequency Bluetooth full-stereo headset, including bass reflex speakers. I can't even imagine anything going beyond this, though I'm sure they'll dream up something, someday.

Continued from page 167

Windshields

That's right, I said windshields. And yes, I ride with one virtually all the time. I shouldn't have to tell you the advantages of one. A well-designed and properly installed windshield can improve aerodynamics, reduce fatigue, provide protection—the list of benefits goes on and on.

A well-designed windshield could be considered the minimum amount of bodywork to make a motorcycle touring-worthy.

I really love the trend toward adjustable shields that you can raise and lower as conditions dictate. But too much of a good thing can be bad, and by that, I mean those ridiculously oversized windshields that have become so popular. In general, I believe you should always be able to look over your windshield if necessary and to duck behind it when you need to. Oversized windshields not only carry the potential to block your view, but they catch a lot more air, and that pressure is transferred to either your frame or your steering head, thus compromising your control of your motorcycle. I remember once talking to a guy with one of those giant shields who told me, "I just really like that big, still air pocket it gives me."

I told him, "Hey, if you really like that sort of thing, I know a windshield that will work even better than the one you've got." When he brightened and looked at me quizzically, I said, "It comes as stock equipment on a Buick."

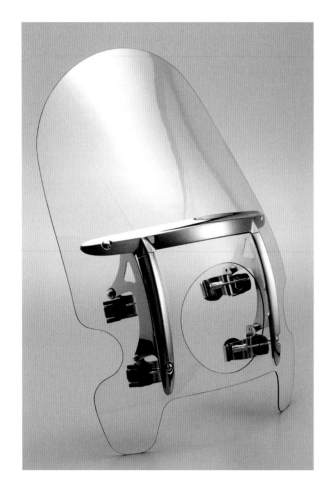

Stereos

There is a long-standing argument among riders about the advantages and disadvantages of listening to music while you're riding. I don't intend to rehash all of that here, but will just say that while I understand the problems of being distracted by music when one should be concentrating on the ride, I also believe that in certain situations, it can save you from the even deadlier distraction of sheer boredom. That being the case, I like having the option of being able to listen to some tunes when the situation merits. By way of a little personal background, I offer another parable from my past, one I call . . .

Intercoms

One of my favorite stories regarding intercom systems, which I've recounted several times at rallies like Americade, is called "Over Here and Over There." Way back in 1975, when my wife and I were fairly new to motorcycle touring, I noticed that we had a real hard time communicating with each other while riding, and decided to do something about it. I had always been a tinkerer in electronic gadgetry, and with about $50 in parts from the local RadioShack, I set about to build us a helmet-to-helmet intercom system. I'm not sure whether you could buy such things ready-built at the time or not. If they existed, I sure hadn't seen one, but I also doubt I was the first to think of or to try building such a device.

My first couple of attempts were dismal failures, but on the third try I came up with a system that actually worked quite well and could be carried in my jacket pocket. A few months later the system got its first trial by fire when we took an extended tour through Utah, Arizona, and Nevada. Mechanically, the unit worked almost perfectly, but it also created a whole new set of problems for me that I hadn't previously considered.

In fairly short order, I began to realize that body language and facial expressions played a very large part in conversation, and when you couldn't see the person you were speaking with, certain difficulties arose. Now, you would think these same problems would arise when speaking on a telephone, but they don't. There are things that come up when you're only a few inches apart that would never be part of a conversation on a telephone. I suppose the best way to explain that is by example.

We were riding across Colorado when I heard my wife's voice in my ear.

"Oh, look! There's a deer!" she said.

"Where?" I replied.

"Over *here*," she yelled.

To which I replied, "Where the heck is 'over here'?"

She responded, "Never mind. You missed it."

"Well," I said, only slightly put out, "for future reference, would you mind explaining what you mean when you say 'over here'? If I can't see where you're looking or pointing, it doesn't mean anything to me."

She said, "I didn't realize it was that difficult. I thought it was understood that 'over here' means to the right, and 'over there' means to the left."

"Believe it or not, dear, I don't recall ever hearing that before. But I promise I won't forget it."

And on we rode in peace and harmony for several hundred more miles until we arrived at the Painted Desert. Then, suddenly . . .

"Oh my, look at the bald eagle on the cactus!"

"Where?" (quick second thought) "Which side?"

"On this side."

(pregnant pause) "Okay, I give up—which side is *this* side?"

"Never mind. You missed it."

Now, keep in mind, we were still pretty much newlyweds at the time, so I was inclined to be much more tolerant than I am today.

"*Ahemmm.* Okay dear, but it would help if you would stick to one description of a direction. I get easily confused. Now, is 'this side' the same as 'over here,' or 'over there'?"

"You're just being difficult. Everyone knows that 'this side' is on your right. '*That* side' is on your left."

"News to me. But whatever you say, dear. I'll file that one away with the other. I promise to try not to be so difficult in the future."

(Just as a side note, guys, in the ensuing years of relating this story to

An intercom system can making riding two-up a much more enjoyable experience. Or not....

large groups of riders, I've found that women find these explanations perfectly understandable. Evidently it's embedded somewhere in their genetic code. Men, on the other hand, are completely clueless in regards to these directional signals.)

My wife was very quiet for the next several hours, punishing me for my ignorance, no doubt. But then she spotted a particularly spectacular sight of some sort, and couldn't restrain herself.

"Wow. Would you look at that!"

"What?"

"That . . . that *view*!"

"Where?"

"On my side."

I spoke without thinking this time. A dangerous thing to do.

"Whaddaya mean *my side*? How am I supposed to know which side of the !@#$%^& bike is *your* side?"

Despite the 90-plus degree temperature out there in the desert, I felt a chill in her reply.

"You know perfectly well that the right side of the bike is my side."

"And how, pray tell, am I supposed to have known that?"

"Because you decided it yourself. Every time we go on a trip, you always pack my stuff in the right saddlebag, and your stuff in the left. Obviously, the right side is my side."

> **My wife was very quiet for the next several hours, punishing me for my ignorance, no doubt. But then she spotted a particularly spectacular sight of some sort, and couldn't restrain herself.**

I had to admit, she had a point. I *did* always pack her stuff on the right side.

"Okay. I give up. You're right. But for the sake of us not killing each other before this trip is over, may I make a suggestion?"

"What?"

"Well, pilots used to have this same problem with communicating directions to each other, and they developed a simple and foolproof way around it. All you have to do is imagine the bike as sitting in the center of a clock face. Now, all directions are the hours displayed around you. Something straight ahead would be at 12 o'clock. Directly right would be 3 o'clock, and to the right but slightly back would be 4 or 5 o'clock. See how it works?"

"I don't know. I'm not sure if I can keep that straight."

"Well, if you have problems imagining the clock face, just look at your watch for reference, okay? All I ask is that you give it a try."

"Okay."

Needless to say, I waited with great anticipation for her next sighting.

I didn't have to wait too long.

"Look at that house up on the hill."

"Where . . . wait a second . . . think about it, remember the clock."

Long pause, then a voice filled with frustration.

"I can't do it. I don't know."

"Just relax and think for a moment. If you can't visualize the clock, look at your watch."

"I tried that. I can't do it. It doesn't work. And it's *your* fault!"

I lost my cool.

"Whaddaya mean it's my fault? I've done everything I could to make it easy for you. How the hell could it be my fault?"

"Well, you're the one that bought me the damn digital watch for Christmas, fool!"

Fast-forward to 2009, when helmet intercom systems are cheap, reliable, and lightweight. Some bikes even come with them built-in as standard equipment, as on the Honda Gold Wing and Harley Electra Glide, but even if they don't, there are both wired and wireless units made by folks like Chatterbox that can be easily installed in your helmets. Or, as in the most recent acquisition for myself and my wife, helmets such as the Nolan N-Com, which feature built-in, wireless intercoms. About the only drawback I've found with such units is remembering that every couple of days, you need to plug your helmet into a charger overnight.

Despite my personal parable of how wrong communications can go, I can't really imagine any argument against using an intercom system if you ride two-up, except that I suppose some people relish the solitude of the ride, and simply don't want to talk to anyone—including their co-rider. But let's face it, when you're riding together, you simply need to communicate at times, if for nothing more than not missing that next rest area exit because someone needs a potty break.

> **I can't really imagine any argument against using an intercom system if you ride two-up, except that I suppose some people relish the solitude of the ride, and simply don't want to talk to anyone—including their co-rider.**

GPS Systems

When portable GPS systems first became available for motorcyclists, I scoffed at them and vowed I would never use one. Not only did I feel fairly confident in my own navigational skills, I had always considered that two of the most enjoyable things about riding were the time spent planning and mapping journeys, and believe it or not, the adventure of getting lost. In addition, I have to admit that I feared that if I ever did start using GPS, my ability to navigate on my own would erode from misuse. I think a good example of that is the current easy access to electronic calculators. Heck, I've even got one in my cell phone! And like everyone else, over the years I began to rely on these cheap and easily accessible devices to do all my multiplication and division for me, until I noticed a few years ago that I was barely capable of even figuring out the tip on a simple dinner bill by myself. I feared that a GPS would have the same kind of effect, so I simply refused to use one.

Then came the day, about five or six years ago, when I flew to Atlanta and borrowed a BMW from a friend there to ride to the Honda Hoot in Tennessee. My friend had installed a Garmin GPS on his bike, but I just figured I wouldn't even bother to turn it on. And I didn't—at least not the first day. But on my second day of meandering almost aimlessly through the back roads of Georgia, it started to rain—hard. Within a few hours, I had lost my bearings completely. Road signs were almost impossible to read through the downpour, and I couldn't

GPS systems may be the most commonly purchased accessory for touring bikes these days, and for good reason. A few bikes, like this top-of-the-line Gold Wing, now come with built-in GPS, but quite frankly I wouldn't recommend going this way. Updating your maps or software, installing routes, building routes, adding items to your database, and other functions are all either impossible or very difficult with a built-in unit. Buy a separate unit and install it yourself on the handlebars or dash. It's cheaper and more efficient, and you can always upgrade to a newer unit later if you want.

One advantage of riding two-up is that you don't have to fight over who gets to use the GPS unit.

even tell where the sun was in the sky, to gauge my approximate direction of travel. I finally stopped under the awning of a deserted gas station and turned on the GPS. Though I'd never used one before, I was surprised at how intuitive the operation was, and within about 10 minutes, I'd programmed a route to my destination in Tennessee, even managing to get the little device to direct me around the big interstate highways that I hate so much.

I was so impressed that when I got back home a few weeks later, I purchased a Garmin StreetPilot and installed it on my bike. And, like any kid with a new toy, I began playing with it incessantly. Soon, I was using the GPS to guide me to places as simple to find as my local gas station and bank, even though I knew perfectly well how to get to those places on my own. It became a game—to see if the Garmin could find a better or quicker route to places than the ones I'd developed on my own. Sure enough, before long I was almost totally dependent on the darned thing. My epiphany came about six months later, as I was sitting on my bike in my own driveway and suddenly realized that I had just spent about a half an hour carefully programming a route into the Garmin, to go to a place that was less than a 20-minute ride away, and which I probably could have ridden to with my eyes closed. I turned the unit off and rode all day without it. The next day, I removed it from my bike.

But when I moved to Connecticut the next year, I suddenly found that I now had a very real need for GPS, and started using it again. Because I was in all-new territory, and knew none of the roads, towns, landmarks, or anything else, having a navigational system was a real blessing. As I began exploring New England, it became an invaluable tool for finding historical sites, such as Revolutionary and Civil War battlefields. I doubt that I would have seen half as much history as I did, if not for the GPS.

Then I moved back to Southern California again, and though I had no need of the Garmin for finding my way around my old stomping grounds, I soon realized that it would be an invaluable tool for running my new touring company. I mean, after all, it's perfectly okay to get lost or make U-turns when you're riding alone or with a buddy, but it's

The Zumo quickly became an indispensable tool for my tour company, especially since my two assistant tour leaders also had them.

very unprofessional (not to mention dangerous) when you're leading a tour of a dozen riders from out of state.

The problem was, by now I had made a GPS convert out of my wife, and we only had the one unit that would transfer from the family car to the bike. When I was off on tour, she didn't want to be without her Garmin, so I had to buy a second unit. Naturally, I bought the newer, fancier unit for my bike—a Garmin Zumo. Not only was the Zumo water- and shock-resistant, with Bluetooth wireless, mp3, XM radio, and the like, but it even had customizable pointers, so you could actually see a little motorcycle cruising down the full-color, three-dimensional road. How cool is that?

The Zumo quickly became an indispensable tool for my tour company, especially since my two assistant tour leaders also had them. After I'd built or modified the daily routes on a tour, I could transfer them directly into their Zumos, so we were always on the same page, even if we lost sight or communication with each other.

But, after only about six months, I suddenly realized I was falling right back into the same old trap again—I was becoming totally dependent on the GPS, and either losing or just ignoring my own navigational instincts and skills.

Recently, I've started to once again make a conscious effort to wean myself from the Garmin teat. I really don't *need* that seductive female voice coaxing me, "In five . . . hundred . . . feet . . . make a left turn." I can make a left turn all on my own, thank you, and maybe . . . just maybe . . . I don't *want* to turn left here. Did you ever think of that? Huh?

It has become a battle of wills, but I *can* get this monkey off my back—really.

In all seriousness, though, a GPS is a fantastic tool that can greatly enhance the pleasures of motorcycle touring. But I find you really do have to look out for becoming too dependent on the darned thing. Don't miss that great little side road or that historical marker just because it isn't in the programmed routing. Turn off the routing and just use the maps, or you can engage in my own personal favorite use for a GPS: lock in your starting point, wherever it might be, and then turn the unit off. Take off and ride wherever the mood takes you, only keeping track of the time. When you're halfway between the time you left and the time you need to be back, turn the GPS back on, and ask it to take you back. Switch the preferences back and forth between "fastest time" and "shortest distance," and compare the routes on the map, looking for the one you like best. You might even want to enable the "avoid highways" preference, and see what it comes up with that way. In any case, whichever route looks the most interesting to you, choose that one, and let the GPS take you back.

If I were to give any advice from my own experiences with GPS, I guess the bottom line would be to use your GPS less as a crutch, or more as a safety net. Remember, it's only a tool.

And if it sounds like I am preaching to myself here—you're exactly right.

Seats and Seat Pads

There was a time when the most popular accessory purchased by touring riders was an aftermarket seat. Motorcycle seats as supplied by the bike manufacturers were woefully inadequate, uncomfortable, and downright painful if you sat on them for more than about an hour at a time. For the most part, that has dramatically improved this past decade, as the OEMs wised up and started paying attention to rider ergonomics. In truth, the original problem was cause by a sales gimmick: original equipment seats were built with overly-soft padding because when the potential buyer first sat on them in the showroom, they felt really good, thus helping sell the bike. Unfortunately, a too-soft seat will pack

> If I were to give any advice from my own experiences with GPS, I guess the bottom line would be to use your GPS less as a crutch, or more as a safety net.

down after an hour or so of sitting on it, and also become less and less cushy each time you ride. They don't provide the proper support, and as they compress and form to your shape, they also don't allow any shift in your body position. You soon develop pressure points and hot spots, resulting in a phenomenon known among riders as "monkey butt."

A good touring seat should be padded, certainly, but with a firm padding that allows both support and movement. It should also be sculpted into a shape that, while providing adequate support for your back and buttocks, is narrowed on the front sides to allow you to put your legs more-or-less straight down when at stops. If it's raised too much on the sides, or has any kind of a hard edge where your thighs cross over, it will restrict the blood flow to your lower legs and feet, a condition that will become most painfully obvious when you step off the bike after riding a few hours.

An extreme simplification of the problem is this: when you're seated, two small round bones called the ischial tuberosities are what you're sitting on. If your seat design allows your weight to concentrate on these two points, you're going to hurt—period. The trick is to distribute your weight evenly, to support you firmly, and to allow a range of motion without sliding all around when the bike brakes or accelerates. It's not as easy as it sounds, but there are a lot of seats out there that are getting pretty good at it.

Once upon a time, the seat on the Honda Gold Wing was considered one of the worst touring seats ever made. Hardly anyone who bought a GL kept the OEM seat, or if they did, they had it modified with covers or pads. Honda

The Airhawk seat pad (below left) is my personal favorite accessory when riding a bike with a seat that just doesn't fit me right. You can adjust the air pressure to whatever degree feels best, and it really reduces pain and fatigue.

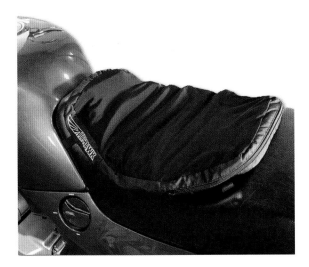

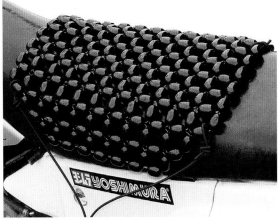

"Ouch!" to some, but "aaahhhh" to others. I can't get used to beaded seat covers, but I know a lot of riders who swear by them.

finally addressed the problem with the GL1500 model, and improved on it even more with the GL1800 model. These days, I'd venture to say that only about 10 percent of Wing owners bother to change out their seats, as opposed to nearly 90 percent back in the 1970s.

And yet, while seat design has improved dramatically, the truth is that no two butts are exactly alike, and there's a fairly good chance you're going to want or need some kind of modification to your stock unit. Buying a custom-fitted aftermarket seat, designed specifically for you, is obviously the ultimate solution, but it comes at an ultimate price, also—usually $750 or more—making it an option for only the most serious or well-heeled riders. For most of us, the best option is a seat pad of some kind.

Seat pads come in four basic types: Beaded, gel-filled, sheepskin, and air bladder.

Beaded Pads

Beaded pads are both the least-expensive and the least-popular of motorcycle seat covers. Probably because the idea just seems so weird. And yet, they actually do work, and those riders who use them will swear by them. The beads are usually made from wood, but sometimes from plastic, strung together with cotton or nylon cord. Basically, they lift your butt a half-inch or so off the seat, allowing air to circulate between the beads. This keeps your butt cooler and allows sweat to evaporate, thus greatly reducing the hot spots and chafing that create monkey butt. The beads also create a sort of massaging effect that improves blood circulation. Personally, I could never adapt to a beaded cover, but I wouldn't suggest counting them out until you've tried one. They can usually be had for around $10 - $15, so it might be worth the investment.

Sheepskin Pads

Sheepskin pads are exactly what they say: the skin of a sheep, with the wool still attached. They tend to stay cool in the summer and warm in the winter (just like they do for the sheep), and they wick away moisture while adding a pleasantly comfortable layer of padding. Sheepskins are very popular as motorcycle seat covers for good reason.

About the only serious drawback I've found is that the thickness needed to get all the benefits also raises your butt about an inch off

> **Personally, I could never adapt to a beaded cover, but I wouldn't suggest counting them out until you've tried one.**

the seat. If you're inseam-challenged like me (29 inches), and already stretching a bit to reach the ground on your bike, this is going to cause a problem.

Gel-filled Pads

Gel-filled pads are just that: nylon seat covers filled with a viscoelastic polymer gel that forms to your butt when you sit on it. They do a great job of distributing your weight evenly, with the drawback that the gel will tend to shift when your weight shifts, which can cause a somewhat uneasy sensation when cornering. The gel is also great at holding its temperature, which can be either a good thing, or a bad one, depending on the situation. If, for example, you leave it on the bike, sitting out in the sun on a summer day, it's going to be hot as hell when get on, and it's going to stay that way for hours. Ditto for if you let it stay on overnight and get cold. It won't warm up for a long, long time. That's why this very same gel is used in hospitals for both heating pads and cold compresses. On the other hand, if you take the pad into your hotel room on a cold night and warm it up, it will keep your butt toasty warm for hours into the next day's ride, and vice-versa for putting it in a refrigerator the night before a hot ride through the desert.

Air-filled Pads

Air-filled pads are, in my opinion, the best of the lot, but they're also the priciest. The technology was originally developed for hospital beds, to prevent bedsores, and consists of neoprene rubber shaped into dozens of little square cells, sort of resembling an egg crate. The space between the cells allows for air circulation, while the cells themselves provide the support. The amount of support can be adjusted simply by blowing more air into the pad through a valve, or letting some out. That way, you can fine-tune the pad to your own personal comfort level. The trick is not to inflate the pad too much, but too find a flotation level, where your butt is suspended about a half-inch above the seat. A good air pad, like the Airhawk, will set you back around $200, but in most cases, I think you'll find it's worth every penny in increased, long-range touring comfort.

Heated Seats and Handgrips

Like most motorcycle accessories, the first heated seats were very expensive, bulky, and quite frankly, not very good. Part of the problem stemmed from the fact that they put a fairly high amperage draw on your electrical system that most bikes simply weren't equipped to handle. But these days, the heating elements can be made much more compact, aren't terribly expensive. In addition, most bikes designed for touring have alternator systems that can easily handle the lower, one to two-amp demands that they require.

> **Most bikes designed for touring have alternator systems that can easily handle the lower, one to two-amp demands that they require.**

Obviously heated seats aren't for everyone, but if you do a lot of touring, they can make a considerable difference in your comfort level. While you might think of them as just something to keep your buns warm, the truth is that, much like a heated vest or jacket liner, when you warm any part of your body, the blood passing through your veins and arteries is going to carry some of that warmth to the rest of your body.

Naturally, the easiest heated seat solution is to buy a unit that's factory-equipped by your bike's manufacturer. Top of the line touring bikes almost always offer this option, but it comes at a premium price. The next best thing is to buy an aftermarket heater that installs under your seat, between the outer cover and the foam padding. Just keep in mind that even the thinnest of these is going to raise your seat height a bit, and probably negate a small amount of the cushioning effect of your padding. In most cases these are negligible trade-offs, but if your seat is already a bit tall for you, or a bit stiff for your tastes, this could push you past your comfort level. You also need to make sure that the heating element and any wiring or connectors needed to hook it up are waterproof.

In most cases, you'll find that a simple on-off switch is not a good idea, but also that a full-range thermostat is overkill. The simplest solution is to have a switch with high-medium-low settings.

Most of the advice for the heated seats can also be applied to heated handgrips, with one important difference: if you're opting for aftermarket heated grips, I would strongly advise purchasing complete grip assemblies with built-in heating elements, like those made by Hot Grips. There are much less expensive wraparound heating elements, that simply go over your existing grips, but in general, using these is a very bad idea. First of all, they change the outer diameter of your grips, making it more difficult to get a firm grip on your handlebars. Secondly, I've found that all of the ones I've tried can and will lose their hold on the grip

> You're riding on the freeway
> in a cold rain, when some idiot
> in the lane to your right suddenly decides
> to swing into your lane without looking.
> There is a car close on your tail,
> so braking hard isn't an option.

and slip at the most inopportune times. Try to imagine this scenario, which actually happened to me: You're riding on the freeway in a cold rain, when some idiot in the lane to your right suddenly decides to swing into your lane without looking. There is a car close on your tail, so braking hard isn't an option. What you need to do is accelerate quickly and swerve into the open lane to your left. You make a sudden twist of your right wrist for full throttle, and the heated cover on your grip slips. Your hand, and the heated cover, rotate down, but the actual throttle grip only goes about a third of the way before the grip's spring tension overcomes the surface tension of the heated cover, and the throttle snaps shut. I was lucky, in that the driver saw me at that exact moment and swerved away. But if he hadn't, I would've been toast. The bottom line is simply this—heated grips are a great invention, but just make sure the actual heating element is underneath the surface you're hanging your life on.

Extra Luggage

In addition to the integrated bike luggage we spoke about in earlier chapters, you may at times need additional packing space. There are many ways to accomplish this, some good, some not so good, and some that are downright stupid or dangerous. It's important that you know the difference.

Tankbags

Tankbags are perhaps the most versatile and utilized system for carrying a bit of extra stuff when you travel. They come in a wide variety of sizes, shapes, and mounting systems, depending on your particular circumstances. In general, you want to look for a tankbag that's expandable and waterproof, and that fits well on your bike without impeding your body or coming into contact with your handlebars during a full-lock maneuver. Most attach to the bike with a strap that loops around the steering head at the front, and another to the frame under the front of the seat. This is usually sufficient for a small to medium bag, but if you're opting for a large bag, you'll probably also need lateral straps, that attach to the sides or under the middle of the tank, as larger bags can become top-heavy when loaded, and could slide around at the worst possible time, such as when making a hard turn. There are also tankbags

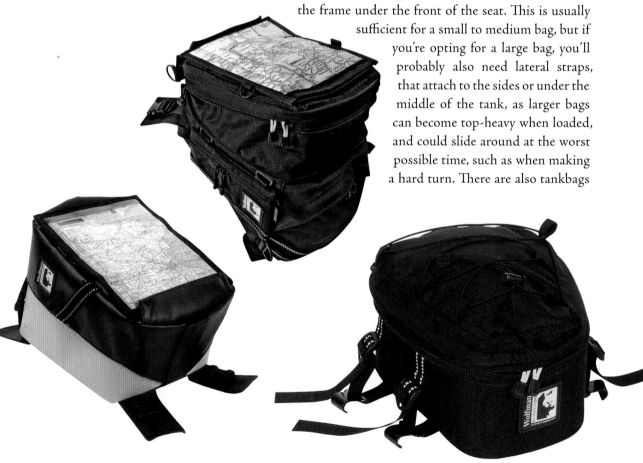

with magnetic mounts, and while I have to admit that I have reservations about trusting my gear to a set of magnets, in reality I've tried a few of these and been very impressed with how secure and stable they were. Advantages of a tankbag are that it keeps things you might need at a moment's notice easily accessible; it places its weight nearest to the bike's center of gravity so that it doesn't impair handling; it's usually easily removable for carrying your stuff away; and most of them have a clear plastic sleeve on top for easy viewing of a map or riding directions.

Tail Packs

Tail packs that attach to the rear seat or a luggage rack at the back of the bike are probably the second-most popular luggage addition, especially for those who tour on sport or sport-touring bikes. They offer more packing space than a tankbag, and carry the weight approximately in the same way you would carry a passenger. Like a tankbag, they should obviously be either waterproof or come with a raincover, and expandability is a big plus. Remember what we told you earlier about how your stuff will inevitably grow as you travel. Another option you might want to consider is buying a tail pack that comes with straps that allow it to be worn as a backpack, for carrying it around with you when off the bike. It's important, however, that you not get carried away with size, particularly in terms of height. The tail pack really shouldn't extend more than about 18 inches

Luggage racks are a good idea if you don't have a topbox (trunk), but make sure they're relatively small and securely mounted through to the bike's frame. I prefer the kind with an attached backrest, like this Stealth model from Pirate's Lair, but whatever you get, make sure it has attachment points for bungies or tie-down straps, like both of these.

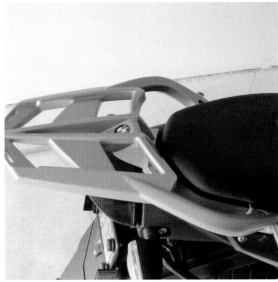

I know I didn't mention deer whistles in this section on accessories, but that's because it would take 10 pages just to explain why they don't work. Take my word for it; these things are a total waste of time and money. Lights, a good horn, and staying alert will serve you much better.

Any good dealership will carry dozens of different kinds of luggage, and you'll find an amazing variety available online. Look for how and where it attaches, and where the weight is going to be carried on the bike. The best luggage is waterproof, lockable, and expandable.

above the seat or luggage rack, and you should be careful to pack your heavier items in the bottom. Always keep your bike's center of gravity in mind.

Trailers

Trailers are a popular option for those who travel two-up for extended periods of time. However, you should always keep in mind that no motorcycle manufacturer produces or recommends the use of a trailer with any of their bikes. Despite most trailer owners' declaration that "you don't even know it's back there," the undeniable truth is that towing a trailer has a considerable effect on your bike's handling characteristics. First of all, having an extra 200 to 400 pounds of inertia pushing against the back of the bike when you brake is obviously going to greatly increase your braking distance, not to mention wearing out your brake pads a lot faster. A trailer is going to make you more susceptible to the effects of crosswinds, have a debilitating effect on your suspension performance on bumps, and the weight on the tongue is going to have a leveraging effect that will lighten your front wheel, thus reducing the friction coefficient of your front contact patch, which is critical for maximum cornering and braking efficiency. For this reason, you need to be extremely careful about the tongue weight, or the

amount of weight that your trailer puts on the ball of the hitch. Think of your bike as a lever, or a child's teeter-totter. When you put weight on the hitch, it's like putting a child on one end of the lever. Your rear wheel axle is the fulcrum in the middle, and your front wheel is the other end of the lever, or teeter-totter. Every ounce of weight you put on the back end is going to result in a lightening of the front end, leveraging weight off your front wheel. But despite all that, as long as you're aware of the need for extra caution and ride accordingly, most larger touring bikes are perfectly capable of handling the implied stresses, and if you really need and want the quantum increase in packing space, nothing beats a trailer.

Hitch-mounted Cases

Hitch-mounted cases are becoming increasingly popular with those who have a trailer hitch on their bike, but at times don't necessarily want or need as much space as a trailer provides. Such things can be a viable alternative, but you need to be very, very careful about the size and weight, keeping both to an absolute minimum. Read what we just wrote about the tongue weight of a trailer. This same warning applies, in spades, to any kind of hitch-mounted luggage case or cooler.

I toured three weeks through the Alps with this little BMW F650 GS and fell in love with its expandable saddlebags. Space when I needed it, but no bulky bags when I didn't.

Chapter 8

Common Pitfalls and Mistakes

Overdoing It

It seems that virtually all of the most common mistakes made by those new to motorcycle touring involve overdoing something. It's important to remember that with touring, as with most other things in life, moderation is often the key. But let us be clear on one thing: I'm not by any means suggesting that you shouldn't aspire to riding farther, or to more exotic locales, than you might have ever dreamed possible. Quite the contrary—you should always go for all the gusto you can get. That's what this sport is all about, after all: trying

You can make the tour a lot more fun for everyone involved if you avoid some common mistakes.

adventures that the majority of the population would consider too risky. It's all about the adventure, but we need to also remember that we do this for the enjoyment, and one of the best ways to maximize that enjoyment is to minimize the hassles.

In that vein, I believe there are three types of overdoing it that most commonly contribute to creating problems on a tour: overplanning, overpacking, and overeating. That being the case, here are my thoughts on each.

Overplanning

Overplanning is probably the easiest trap for a touring motorcyclist to fall into, mostly because the planning of a trip can often be such an enjoyable pastime—especially if you live in a climate that forces you to put your bike away for several months every year. It's during these downtimes that a rider often quenches his or her cabin fever by poring over maps and travel brochures, meticulously plotting a great adventure for the coming riding season. This

A regimented itinerary can turn a fun trip into the Bataan Death March. Make sure to allow for plenty of leisure time and spontaneous activity.

If you're not a slave to a schedule you'll have the freedom to explore the places you travel through.

allows us to become mentally involved in a ride, even when we're prevented from participating in the actual, physical reality.

I am certainly not saying that you should give up this activity—it's a great mental exercise and stress reliever—but what you have to be careful of is locking yourself into a plan so rigidly that sticking to your schedule becomes the primary focus of the tour, instead of actually enjoying the ride. Just the other day I met a couple who'd recently returned from a tour in Utah. When they told me they had spent the night in Torrey, on their way to Moab, I said, "Oh great! Then you got to ride up Highway 12! Isn't that one of the greatest motorcycle roads in the world?"

To which the man replied, "No, we had a schedule to keep, to get to our motel room in time to do laundry that night, so we had to take the faster route up Highway 89."

I was stunned, but tried not to show it. Here were two people who had ridden thousands of miles for their once-in-a-lifetime motorcycle tour of one of the most scenic places on the planet, and they had skipped one of the all-time great motorcycle roads so that they could keep to their pre-arranged schedule. They had allowed the plan to take priority over the purpose of the trip, and though I'm sure they were glad that they got their laundry done that afternoon, they had no idea how badly they had cheated themselves.

I've planned literally hundreds of tours for myself alone, for me and my wife, for friends, and professionally for large and small groups. From that experience, I'd like to share a couple of tips about planning your personal motorcycling adventure. In general, though, just try to remember one simple thing, which has been the touring motorcyclist's mantra for as long as people have been riding: "It ain't the destination, it's the journey."

Well-designed luggage can make touring not only easier for you, but also for your significant other.

Packing items your significant other may need at the bottom of a top-loading saddlebag means that he or she won't be able to reach those items until you unpack. This is not a recipe for domestic bliss.

Don't get obsessed with mileage. Just because you know you're capable of riding 400 miles per day doesn't mean you should plan your tour around that number. In fact, you should probably take the number of miles you feel comfortable with and reduce that by 30 percent for your tour. Remember, this is a vacation, and probably through unknown territory. You're going to want and need extra time for sightseeing and photo stops, for lunch at that neat little diner you spotted, for talking to folks you meet at rest stops, and if you're lucky, maybe to even get lost now and then. In fact (and this is the way I plan my professional tours), you're better off ignoring mileage completely and

trying to plan your trip by hours in the saddle. Factor about 30 mph for back roads, 40 for state highways, and 50 for interstates (which should be avoided whenever possible), which is a pretty good rule of thumb for including time needed for rest and gas stops, and then plan your route for approximately six hours per day of actual saddle time.

Tip Number 2

Don't get locked into hotel or campground reservations. Sure, I make reservations ahead of time. Sometimes weeks ahead, and sometimes just the day before. But in most cases, those reservations can be cancelled right up until about 4:00 pm the day you're scheduled to arrive, without any penalty. If weather, road conditions, or any number of other factors are delaying you, just call and cancel. Unless it's a holiday weekend in a well-traveled tourist area, you can always find something else that will be in a location or timeframe that's more convenient to your newly adjusted schedule. I have to admit that on occasion, that has meant spending a night in less than desirable lodgings, but it's also true that it has just as often resulted in finding a really neat little out-of-the-way spot that was really enjoyable. Remember—this is supposed to be an adventure!

Tip Number 3

Too many cooks spoil the broth. If you're traveling alone, obviously there isn't going to be a conflict with planning. The same will probably be true if you're traveling with a friend. But once the trip starts to involve three or more riders, look out. Before you even start planning the tour, your first decision should be who is in charge. That doesn't mean you need to elect an absolute dictator,

Before you even start planning the tour, your first decision should be who is in charge.

but it really should be understood that one person is the tour leader and the final decision-maker, particularly when it comes to routing and scheduling. Without that understanding up front, I can practically guarantee one or more roadside arguments, which will not only eat up time, but strain relationships. Your tour leader not only needs to be someone ready and willing to listen to suggestions on changing the itinerary on the fly, but also someone who can and will put his foot down, when necessary, and keep the group on plan. This also relates to the next tip, when staying the course may not be the wisest option.

Continued on page 198

The Trophy Wife

Once, a few years ago, when I was running a motorcycle rental office in New England, I rented a Gold Wing to a couple who were going out on a five-day ride. The man told me he'd been riding for about 10 years, but was taking along his new fiancée, who had only been riding for a couple of weeks and who had never been out on the road for more than a day at a time. And in fact, though the man had ridden before, it turned out that this was to be his first time out for more than a weekend.

After we finished all the paperwork, I took them out to the bike for a quick orientation, as neither had ever ridden anything but a Harley cruiser.

Things seemed to be going along fairly well until they started unloading their luggage from the car they had come in, and piling it up next to the bike. It was immediately evident to me that they had brought along about three times as much gear as even a Gold Wing, with its capacious, integrated luggage, would be able to carry. I could see the handwriting on the wall—especially when the woman reached into the car trunk and pulled out four extra pairs of shoes and one of those giant, 1,500-watt hair-dryers. And the guy wasn't looking much better as he unloaded his laptop computer, cowboy hat, cigar humidor, and a portable amplifier system for his iPod.

You never really know a person until you've spent a couple of weeks sharing a motorcycle saddle together. If your relationship can survive that, you've found true love.

I tried, as tactfully as possible, to explain to them that they were going to need to leave at least two-thirds of their stuff behind, but they were having none of that. As soon as the man saw the reaction to my statement on his new girlfriend's face—a face which, by the way, was at least 15 years younger than his own—he assured her that he was prepared for this eventuality and had brought along plenty of bungie cords and bags for strapping everything onto the bike. So I left them to their devices, and retreated back into my office.

About an hour later I wandered back out to the parking lot, to a scene I'll never forget. The Gold Wing now had stuff sacks bungied on top of each saddlebag, the tank, underneath the trunk, and three deep on top of the trunk, sticking up about two feet above the back of the passenger backrest. Despite all that, there were still two more bags sitting on the ground beside the bike, and the couple was engaged in a rather heated discussion about what was to be left behind. The man was arguing—logically, I thought—that at least two pair of the woman's high-heeled dress shoes could be left back. She in turn was informing him that he'd promised to take her out someplace nice for dinner along the way, and that she would rather be caught dead than to wear tennis shoes or motorcycle boots into a fancy restaurant.

As much as I hated to add fuel to the rising flames, I really felt that I needed to step in and inform the couple that their method of packing was very likely to scuff the paint on the bags, trunk, and tank of the brand-new Wing, and if that occurred, I would be holding their $1,000 damage deposit to pay for repairing the paint. The girlfriend's reaction to that statement, which I really thought I made as

diplomatically as possible, was to inform her beau that if he had to leave behind one more item of hers, that he may as well leave her behind also, and **permanently**. Seeing the look on her face, and remembering the old adage that discretion is the better part of valor, I decided to remove myself from the area as quickly as possible, and left the poor guy to his fate.

Back in my office once again, I reflected on how lucky I was to be married to woman with several decades of motorcycling behind her, and who was eminently proficient at packing for a tour. Of course, I always hassle her that she's packing too much, but somehow, it always seems to just barely fit into the space on whatever bike we're riding at the time. It's a rare and wonderful talent.

My two rental customers returned five days later. Their body language and facial expressions as they dismounted the bike told me that much of whatever romance they might have once had in their relationship had been left behind somewhere on the road. I tried to make idle, pleasant conversation as they unpacked, but only heard grumblings about "taking two hours every morning to pack the bike, and another hour every evening to unpack." I also gathered that they had not been able to see many of the sights they'd planned on, or eat at the restaurants they'd wanted to, for fear of letting the bike out of their sight and having their excess, bungied-on luggage stolen.

Some people might not think that something as simple as packing right, and packing light, could be a major consideration in how much enjoyment you can get from a motorcycle tour. But we know better—right?

Continued from page 195
Tip Number 4

Have alternate routes in mind. Don't try going over that mountain pass if the ranger says it's snowing up there, just because it's part of your planned route. Ditto for being flexible enough to go around road construction, traffic jams, or bad weather. Is it really worth being miserable just to keep to your schedule? Planning is a good thing, but you also need to be ready and willing to make adjustments as you go, even if it's something as minor as spotting a road sign directing you to some interesting sight previously unknown to you. If it's not too far off the route, and seems worth the effort as long as you're in the area already, go for it. Remember, we do this because it's fun!

Overpacking

From my own experience running guided tours, it seems that the second most common mistake I see riders new to touring making is overpacking.

Like most seasoned motorcycle travelers, my wife and I have developed a system over the years that works perfectly for us. Of course, our basic riding gear never needs to be packed, as we wear the same riding jackets, boots, pants, and gloves almost every day. To this we add a couple of Frogg Toggs rainsuits, because they pack up so small, and two Air Vantage inflatable vests, to go under the jackets if the weather turns cold. We pack a clean change of underwear for every other day (a little more on that later), a couple of T-shirts and a sweatshirt, a pair of shorts and one pair of decent-looking cotton pants, a pair of jeans, and either a pair of sneakers or sandals for wearing off the bike. We find that's sufficient for either a week-long trip, or two weeks if we stop and do laundry somewhere around the halfway point.

> **From my own experience running guided tours, it seems that the second most common mistake I see riders new to touring making is overpacking.**

On rare occasions, when the trip would involve needing extra clothes for special events or extreme weather conditions, we have been known to pick a hotel or a friend's house somewhere along the halfway point, and to ship a box of extra clothing ahead of us. That way, we can just switch the clean stuff for the dirty, and send the box back home, to be waiting for us when we get back.

Of course, we've both also had to learn to make certain compromises. Though I would rather she not pack a hairdryer, my wife insists on having her own along, but has managed to procure a small, fold-up model that takes up very little space. As for myself, you've probably noticed from my pictures that I am rarely without my Australian Outback hat, but years ago I found a crushable version; it can literally be rolled up to about the size of a baseball and still spring back to shape when unpacked. I can always stuff that down into some unused corner of a saddlebag, where nothing else can fit.

Then, of course, we use those tiny, travel-sized containers for all of our toiletries, and have also learned that a lot of smaller, miscellaneous items can be carried in the many pockets of a good riding jacket. In all, it's a very workable system, and we've met many other seasoned bike travelers with variations that we've adapted to ourselves over the years. We've become so efficient with our routine that, with almost no notice or planning in advance, we can have the bike packed and ready to roll out for a tour in about 30 minutes.

> ### Probably the easiest way to begin preparing yourself for a stress-free packing experience is to first look at or make a list of every item you intend to carry along.

Probably the easiest way to begin preparing yourself for a stress-free packing experience is to first look at or make a list of every item you intend to carry along. After that, start asking yourself a few questions about why you need it, whether it's truly essential, and perhaps most importantly, can it be replaced with something that's either smaller and lighter, or can serve more than one purpose.

For example, one of the bulkiest items you can carry is a jacket, and yet some riders try to carry two or even three. I've literally ridden around the world with only one jacket—a lightweight mesh with full body armor. To augment this, I either carry an inflatable, waterproof liner for the cold and wet, or an electrically heated liner and the aforementioned Frogg Toggs. Either of these options takes less than half the packing space of carrying another, separate jacket, while still providing me with everything I need for almost any kind of weather.

Do you really need three or four pair of gloves for differing weather conditions? Why not a good pair of lightweight riding gloves, with rain and windproof liners or covers to slip on? Are you carrying a 12-ounce bottle of shampoo, when you know you aren't going to use more than about 4 ounces during the trip? Same goes for toothpaste, mouthwash, and other toiletries.

Continued on page 202

Parable:
The Run(s)

I was really looking forward to this ride. I was meeting up with an old friend who lived on the Olympic Peninsula in Washington, and he was taking me for a three-day journey to visit all of his favorite roads in the Cascade Mountains. I had ridden a bit in this area in the past on my own, but having a guide who has lived all his life in a region, and is a dedicated motorcyclist, is always the best way to see just about any place you can name.

Dave and I took off early—around 5:45—and knocked off a tank of gas before stopping for breakfast. That's another thing I like about him—he practices the same sort of riding regimen I'm used to. Anyway, the restaurant he planned on stopping at happened to be closed for some reason, so we had to pick out another, unfamiliar place to stop. As I puzzled over the menu, Dave ordered something called a "Fiesta Mexicana Breakfast." When I asked what that was, the waitress said it was eggs mixed with ground beef and salsa. "Sounds good. Give me the same."

When the breakfasts came, they were a bit more gnarly-looking than I had expected. Lots of green chilis and onions and other rather nasty-looking stuff swimming in a shallow pool of grease stared back at me from the plate. I had second thoughts and considered asking the waitress to take it back and bring me some plain old ham and eggs, but seeing that Dave was already attacking his plate with gusto, and knowing he wouldn't like waiting around for me to get a second breakfast, I decided

to go ahead, and dug into the spicy mess. It actually tasted pretty good, but it took two glasses of ice water to put out the fire in my mouth before climbing back on the bike.

Anyway, about two hours down the road I began to feel a slight rumbling in my gut. If you're over about 40 years old, you know what I mean: a harbinger of greater things to come.

Sure enough, within another 20 minutes or so, the rumbling was taking on cataclysmic proportions, and I knew without a doubt I would be in need of a public sanitary facility very soon. But, as Dave and I had no means of communications between our bikes, I needed to catch up with him and signal my need for a pit stop. I opened up the throttle a bit and began gaining on him, but just as I was about to come alongside, he suddenly sped up and pulled away. I increased my speed again, and the scenario repeated again—just as I got close, he pulled away.

"Dammit," I thought, "he thinks I want to play."

I tried flashing my lights and honking my horn, only to find out my horn wasn't working (when's the last time you tried yours, really?). Finally I gave up, and simply decided that as soon as I saw a place where I might find a restroom, I was going to pull off. Dave would notice eventually and come back looking for me, I was sure.

I was really starting to get desperate when I

spotted a small cluster of buildings up ahead, and a gas station sign. Knowing I was but minutes from soiling my best pair of riding pants, not to mention giving Dave a couple of years' worth of campfire stories to tell, I nailed the throttle and shot up to almost 100 miles per hour, fixated on the Mobil sign. Oddly enough, I still didn't catch up with Dave, who must have been going well over the ton when I saw his right blinker come on. Thank goodness! He was heading in for gas.

But as we shot into the deserted-looking station, Dave turned away from the pumps to the side of the building, where he proceeded to skid to a stop and jump off his bike like it was on fire. Without removing his helmet or gloves, he sprinted for the men's room door, beating me to it by seconds and slamming the door in my face.

As I stood outside, jumping from one foot to the other and trying not to think about my situation, I realized that the Mexicana breakfast had claimed more than one victim.

As Dave stepped out of the men's room, with a look of great relief on his face, he began to speak. "Boy, was I ever . . ." Before he could finish, I shoved him unceremoniously out of the way and dove headfirst into sanctuary . . . and salvation.

This scenario was to be repeated in more or less the same fashion for the rest of the day, as we leapfrogged from one restroom to another across Washington State. At one point, as we rode into a very, very small community, once again in mutual dire straits, we were chagrined to notice there was no sign of any public facilities. Without hesitating, I rode up and stopped in front of a small brick building with a sign that said "Town Hall." Without bothering to take the key from my bike, but removing my helmet so I wouldn't look like some kind of two-wheeled terrorist, I jumped off and ran through the front door to find a young receptionist presiding over what appeared to otherwise be a totally empty office. In my best rapid-fire auctioneer voice I announced to the startled young lady— "Excusememiss, we'retravelingthroughyourtownan dneedarestroom—RIGHT AWAY! Canyouhelpus— pleeeeease?"

To her credit, she immediately comprehended the problem, and speaking as rapidly as I as she jumped up from behind the desk, she announced— "Thetoiletsareoutback—GoaroundthebuildingandI'll meetyouwiththekeys!"

This time I beat Dave to the men's room door, but being less attuned to the social proprieties than I, he simply ran straight into the ladies' room.

Okay, it's not the prettiest touring story, but it taught me a lesson once and for all—I'm not 20 years old anymore, and I can't abuse my body like I once did and expect to get away with it. I still pay careful attention to my riding gear and my bike, to make sure they're up to the task at hand. I replace worn tires before they become dangerous. I check my brakes and hydraulics regularly. I get a new helmet when the old one gets damaged. But let's not forget that the most critical piece of riding equipment—the one most responsible for our safety and comfort and ultimate enjoyment of the ride—is also the one we often tend to ignore and abuse the most: our bodies.

Stay healthy—Ride long.

Continued from page 199

If you're going to be out for six or seven days, do you try to carry six or seven changes of socks and underwear? Would it really be that much of a hardship if you only packed three changes, then took 10 minutes after the third day to wash them out in the sink? I do it as soon as I've stopped for the night, then hang them up in front of the motel room's furnace vent to dry overnight. By morning, I've got enough clean underwear to last me the rest of the trip.

The tendency is to think that each of these things (with the exception of the jackets) doesn't really take up much space, and you would be correct in assuming that none of them, taken individually, is really going to make much difference. But taken all together, they can easily add up to the difference between a successful packing experience, and an extremely frustrating one.

I realize that to anyone who has been touring for a while, this advice seems very basic, and so simplistic that it almost goes without saying. What we tend to forget, though, is that each of us has developed our own packing system through dozens of different periods of trial-and-error. The purpose of this chapter, and in fact this whole book, is to help those new to our sport to leapfrog over many of those hard-learned lessons, thus avoiding the problems they can cause. Which brings us to . . .

Overeating

Eating and riding go together like, well . . . eating and riding. Many years ago when I was an officer with the GWRRA, we used to joke that the acronym actually stood for "Gold Wing Restaurant Reviewers Association." It wasn't far from the truth.

One of the great joys of motorcycle touring is finding those really interesting, out-of-the-way places to eat along the way. In fact, you'll find that most motorcycle club runs involve riding to a favorite restaurant, or staging some kind of cookout or picnic at the end of a ride.

One of the great joys of motorcycle touring is finding those really interesting, out-of-the-way places to eat along the way.

But while stuffing yourself with really great barbeque or other such fare at the end of a day trip may be one of life's little pleasures, it's definitely not a good idea when you're in the middle of an extended tour. And, as much as I hate to have to say it, that admonition gains greater significance for every birthday past 40 that you've counted. Gastric distress is never a good thing at any time, but it takes on a whole new meaning when it strikes you on a bike, far from home, as in this embarrassing personal experience . . .

Something Old, Something New

Something Old

This part pretty much goes without saying, but just in case, let's be clear; it's just plain stupid to take off on a tour with old, worn tires on your bike. Check the wear bars before you go, and make sure you have sufficient tread remaining to make the distance planned. That part should be easy and self-evident, but there is another factor concerning your tires that's often overlooked, beyond worn tread or uneven wear patterns like cupping, and that's the tire's age. Motorcycle tires are primarily made from organic compounds, meaning they degrade, or rot, as they get older. Even worse, this rotting takes place mostly from the inside out, meaning it may not be visible to you when inspecting them. This rotting process makes the tire compound lose its flex, which is critical to handling, and causes it to wear much faster than a newer tire. When the rotting reaches a stage where it's evident from the exterior, such as when you see evidence of cracking in the sidewalls, the tire has reached a critically dangerous stage, where it could literally fly apart with no warning—usually at the worst possible time, like when you're in a high-speed cornering situation.

Though the rate of degradation from aging varies a great deal depending on how the tire was stored, both before and after purchase, the climate where

Continued on page 206

With such a small contact patch, you want to make sure your tires are the best available. When there's that little rubber meeting the road, you want to make darn sure that it's good rubber.

Parable:

The Riding Buddy

As touring motorcyclists, the most important relationships we will form in our lives, outside of family, will be that of our touring partners, or riding buddies. We all have friends that we like to ride with, among which are usually a few that we even enjoy riding with for days at a time. But the rarest thing of all is a true riding buddy—a person or a couple that you can not only tolerate riding with, but actually look forward to spending virtually every moment with for weeks on end. In a sense, it's a relationship that's very much like a marriage, without the romance. You have to like riding at approximately the same pace, over the same kinds of roads. You need to agree on the time you like to start in the mornings, and when you want to stop at night. To avoid anyone having to make undue compromises, you're going to have to be satisfied with the same kinds of hotel rooms and restaurants, and if you're going to be sharing a room—which is the only practical way to travel—then you're probably even going to have to agree on what TV shows to watch at night, and what temperature the room thermostat should be set at. I suppose you could boil this all down to just being compatible, but it seems to me that it goes even deeper than that. In many ways, it's the same sort of relationship you often see formed among police or firefighters, or those in a military combat situation. As the months and years pass, and the miles roll up, you'll either drift slowly apart, or, if you're lucky, the bond will only become stronger. To me, my riding buddy Phil has become much more like a brother than a friend. And for this, I count myself very lucky.

A perfect riding relationship like this, it seems to me, can develop in one of several ways. Ideally, it involves virtually no compromise on either side. But for this to happen, the two riders need to mesh almost perfectly, which is a very rare occurrence. Almost as good is when the wants and needs of the two riders come very close, and neither minds making a few minor compromises here and there. That's probably the most common riding buddy relationship. The third,

Few things in life can compare to the thrill of traveling across the country on a motorcycle in the company of good friends.

and to my mind the hardest to find, is the one I have with my buddy Phil. In this relationship, you need to find someone who not only meshes almost perfectly with your own mindset about riding, but who has the kind of personality that always makes the best of whatever life throws at him. Since I've been known to be moody, and at times downright confrontational, Phil makes a perfect buffer between me and whatever problems might arise on the road. In hard-luck situations involving the weather, or bike breakdowns, or whatever, when I tend to get angry and frustrated, Phil always manages to have a smile, to crack a joke about it, and to lift my spirits. I wish I could say that I do the same for him, but I know that isn't true. Phil is a giver and I'm a taker, and I suppose that's the bottom line.

I think it would be safe to say that in my riding career I've known and ridden with more than 10,000 other motorcyclists. Out of those, I count a grand total of four as my best riding buddies. That doesn't mean I don't like anyone else, or want to ride with others—only that these few are the ones I would ride with week after week, year after year, for any amount of time or distance.

As I said, I've been extremely fortunate in my life to have found four really good riding buddies. One passed away nearly 10 years ago, after over a dozen years of us riding together, and the other two live more than 3,000 miles away, one in Eastern Canada and one in New Jersey, so we don't get to ride together nearly as often as we would like. The Canadian's name is Marc Souliere, and my friend in New Jersey is Billy Bigelow.

Sometimes I like to ride all alone. Often, I like to ride with just my wife. Both of these have given

me wonderful and memorable riding experiences. But I'd be lying if I didn't say that my favorite of all is when I'm on the road with one of these good friends at my side. It's an aspect of motorcycling that's often ignored, or at least one that we don't really talk about. We all talk about the great roads, restaurants, and destinations, the bikes we've loved, the rallies, and even such mundane things as favorite accessories and riding gear, but we rarely speak of one of the most important elements of all—the friends we find and the lifelong companionships that are built around our riding.

Whether your riding buddy is on his or her own bike or sharing the seat with you, you'll have a special bond with that person.

Continued from page 203

you live, heat, humidity, and other factors, in general you don't want tires on your bike that are over five years old, and you don't want to purchase tires that are over three years old. Unfortunately, sometimes tires end up being stored in a warehouse or back room for years before they're sold. This is often true of those sold at discount prices by mail order or over the Internet. Be smart: *Don't buy tires unless you can physically examine them in person first.* When you do, look for either a four-digit number stamped into the sidewall by itself, or a series of numbers following the letters "DOT," also stamped into the sidewall. If it's a series of numbers, all you're concerned with are the last four digits. These four numbers, or the four stamped by themselves, represent the actual week and year of the tire's manufacture. For example, if the four digits are 2809, the tire was built in the 28th week of 2009. The newer the tire, the more flexible and resilient, and the better the control and tread life will be. Don't think you're saving money when a dealer offers a 20 percent discount on a tire that's already three or four years old, because the tread will actually wear out at least 20 percent faster than that of a brand-new tire. Let the fools who didn't read this book buy those, while you insist on new rubber.

And finally, in terms of old problems, another that should be self-evident: if you normally change your oil every 3,000 miles, it's been 2,000 since your last change, and you're leaving this week on a 2,500-mile tour, get the oil changed before you go. That is unless you're dead certain there's someplace along the way to get it done, and you don't mind taking the time out of your vacation to see to it.

Something New

I think that perhaps the most common error committed by touring riders, both new and seasoned, is leaving on an extended tour with almost any kind of brand-new, untried equipment. This is particularly true of personal riding gear, like helmets, boots, jackets, gloves, or even sunglasses. Many times, problems with new equipment won't manifest themselves until you've been using the gear for a while, and if you're stuck with that particular piece of gear for the next several days, or even weeks, minor problems will quickly become major ones. For example, that brand-new helmet that seemed to fit okay when you tried it on at the dealership may pinch your ears or chafe your neck, or create uncomfortable hot spots on your forehead after wearing it for six or seven hours. If you're going to have to live with it for seven or eight hours a day, day after day, the discomfort is going to only get worse with each passing hour.

It will become a painful distraction that can ruin the whole trip. The same general advice holds true with gloves that cramp your fingers when gripping the throttle, a jacket collar that chafes your neck, boots that pinch your toes, or even sunglasses that don't fit properly through your helmet lining and rub the area behind your ears raw.

If you're going to buy new gear for a tour, buy it weeks ahead and give yourself time to live with it on several day trips before committing to a long-term relationship. Either that, or use your old tried-and-true equipment for now and save the new stuff until you've had time to break it in. You'll be happier in the long term—trust me.

And finally, another important new thing you probably don't want along on a tour is a new riding companion. I know that sounds harsh, and a bit cold, but years of experience have taught me, the hard way, that it's an almost-universal truth.

Above left: At a major motorcycle rally in the East a couple of years ago, a tire manufacturer was offering free tire inspections. The idea was to try to sell new tires to anyone who needed them, but even the promoters were astounded when, by the end of only the first day, they had identified over 100 bikes wearing tires that didn't meet safety standards. Without a doubt, the biggest failing among riders is forgetting to check the condition of their tires. Don't let that happen to you. Above right: When buying new tires, always look for the date of manufacture, which will be a four-digit number stamped into the sidewall, usually just after the end of the DOT registration number. On this tire it's 0508, meaning this tire was built in the fifth week (first week of February) of 2008. In general, tires have a shelf life of at least five years, but personally, I wouldn't buy one that was over three years old, because I wouldn't know how it was stored during that time.

Bad Advice

I don't remember exactly where or when this took place, but several years ago I was at some kind of motorcycle safety conference when I heard a speech by someone representing the Insurance Institute for Highway Safety (IIHS). For those of you unfamiliar with this outfit, it's a large PR and lobbying agency funded by the major insurance companies. To say that the IIHS has an anti-motorcyling bias would be a major understatement. Anyway, in this particular speech, the IIHS representative made the point that rider education programs were not only useless, but that they had research indicating that they might actually be harmful, and a contributing factor to rising motorcycle accident rates. Their contention was that if a rider was trained to avoid road and traffic hazards, the training somehow imbued them with a false sense of self-confidence, thereby subconsciously encouraging them to take more and greater risks when riding than they might otherwise have if they hadn't gone through the training.

I suppose, with some insane stretch of convoluted logic, some people might actually be able to see some kind of truth to that, but to me it just sounded like one of the stupidest things I'd ever heard, and I told the IIHS rep just that. In fact, I suggested that if he really believed the crap he was spouting, perhaps for his flight back home from the conference he should try to find an airline pilot who had absolutely no flight safety training. This, by his own reasoning, would ensure that the pilot would not expose him or the other passengers to any unnecessary risks. I'm sorry to say he did not respond to my reasoning, but just scowled and turned away.

Just recently I saw this same stupid theory, in a slightly modified form, crop up on one of those Internet bulletin boards about motorcycling. This time, some guy was expounding on the idea that wearing a motorcycle helmet somehow imbued the rider with what he called "Superman Syndrome." Like the IIHS rep's take on safety training, this theory says that if you wear a helmet, it gives you a false sense of confidence and a feeling of invulnerability, which

Though the big BMW adventure touring bikes can traverse rugged terrain in the hands of a skilled pilot, they are too big for serious off-road riding.

in turn results in increased risk-taking and, of course, greater accident rates. Now I'm not in favor of mandatory helmet laws, but I do believe in wearing a helmet when I ride. To me it's a matter of personal choice, and a freedom that I enjoy as an American citizen. But I certainly wouldn't use a stupid argument like this to try to convince someone else not to wear a helmet. In fact, I might suggest that if this theory held any water, then the same could be said for wearing leather chaps, armored jackets, gloves, eye protection or even motorcycle boots. If wearing protective gear gives a rider a false sense of invulnerability, then it stands to reason that we should mandate that all riders henceforth only be allowed to operate their machines when buck naked. That way, none of us would ever take any unnecessary risks, right?

In addition, I have a serious problem with several beginning riding courses, including those taught by the national MSF, which rely heavily on what they call "peer teaching experiences." Along with the National Highway Traffic Safety Administration (NHTSA), the MSF admits that their Basic Riding Course (BRC) is only designed to teach a newcomer the basics of shifting, braking, throttle, and turning, and that they assume that the rider will learn the other, necessary street survival skills through peer-to-peer exchanges with experienced riders. While that may all sound well and good, and I'll be the first to admit there is often much to learn from more seasoned riders, what if the knowledge being passed along is bogus? How do you know that the grizzled old veteran tutoring you isn't just regurgitating some old wives' tales he picked up from someone else decades before? Heck, just a couple of days before writing this, I was sitting in a diner where I overheard an older rider explaining to a newbie that he "needed to get some ape-hanger handlebars on the bike, because it will make it handle better." And the kid was nodding his head! Could anyone really believe something so ridiculous? You bet. I even fell for some of that old lore myself, many years ago.

Back around 1970 I attended one of my first-ever motorcycle rallies in Denver, Colorado. There, while sitting at a picnic table with a bunch of veteran riders who had just learned I was a rookie, I received my initial stock of motorcycling wisdom. I'm sure they all meant well as they spent the afternoon educating me on the following:

> How do you know that the grizzled old veteran tutoring you isn't just regurgitating some old wives' tales he picked up from someone else decades before?

Avoid using the front brake whenever possible.

In a panic situation it will only cause you to be thrown over the handlebars. (*Truth: On virtually all motorcycles, the front brake provides upwards of 70 percent of your available stopping power, and thus is absolutely essential to your survival in a panic situation. When braking, the weight of the rider and bike shifts forward, increasing traction in the front and reducing it in the rear. The harder your stop, the better the front brake works, as the rear becomes less and less effective.*)

Buy fingerless gloves.

Otherwise, you won't be able to feel the bike's controls. (*Truth: Good motorcycle gloves are thinnest where your fingers come in contact with the controls, allowing all the feel you'll ever need, and are padded or armored on the backs and knuckles. In almost any accident that removes the rider from the bike, your fingers become the most vulnerable part of your body. The most common serious injury among professional motorcycle racers is the loss of one or more fingers.*)

If the law allows, don't wear a helmet.

If it's a law, get one of those little skullcaps. A regular helmet will take away your peripheral vision, so you can't see cars coming from the side; makes it difficult to hear; and in warm weather will cause your brain to overheat. (*Truth: A multitude of scientific tests have proven that a quality motorcycle helmet not only doesn't reduce your peripheral vision, it allows you to hear better, and actually reduces your head temperature on hot days.*)

Pull the baffles out of your mufflers.

If your bike is too quiet, car drivers won't hear you coming and will run you down. (*Truth: This is the biggest and perhaps most-commonly repeated fallacy in motorcycling. I could write a whole book just on this one subject, but for now, just remember this: The most recent study of motorcycle accidents reported that "90 percent of all vehicular risks to the rider were in front of the rider prior to the accident." Obviously, noise radiating from the rear of your bike isn't going to help. If someone really believes this, ask them why they don't just tape down their horn button? It would obviously be a lot more effective than loud pipes.*)

In almost any kind of emergency situation, you're better off "laying the bike down" and bailing out, than you are trying to brake or swerving.

(*Truth: Once the bike is down, you've lost all control, and all options as to the final outcome of the crash. But most importantly, consider this: the traction coefficient of* rubber on pavement is about 20 times greater than that of steel or plastic, ergo, if an impact is inevitable, you're going to hit a whole lot faster and harder after laying it down that you would have had you kept your tires on the pavement.)

To keep from overheating (which will cause you to lose your concentration), when riding in the heat, wear only a T-shirt, and maybe even shorts.
(*Truth: I can't tell you how many riders I've had to rescue in the desert because they believed this. Covering up lowers your skin temperature, allows your sweat glands to do their job, reduces dehydration, and helps prevent sunburn. Think of this: Every civilization native to hot climates, such as the nomadic tribes of the Sahara or the Native American tribes of the Southwestern deserts, wears native costumes that involve loose clothing covering virtually every square inch of skin.*)

When going around a low-speed turn, drag your feet so you can catch the bike if it starts to fall over.
Same for when starting out or coming to a stop. (*Truth: This little tidbit has probably been responsible for more serious injuries than any other among motorcyclists. First, removing your feet from the footpegs unbalances the bike, resulting in loss of control. The closer in to the body of the bike our legs remain, the easier the bike is to control. Secondly, if the bike does start to fall over, there isn't a human knee or ankle in existence capable of stopping it. All you'll get for your trouble is at least a serious sprain, or more likely, a broken ankle or permanently disabled knee. Either use the throttle to try to power out of the fall, or just let it go. You'll probably get a few bruises and damage your bike, but it's better than six months on crutches followed by a lifetime of limping.*)

Having a couple of beers before a ride will help you stay loose.
In the event of an accident, your injuries will be less severe, because you didn't tense up. (*Truth: Do I really need to say this? Alcohol slows your reflexes and impairs your judgment! Motorcycling is a concentration-intensive activity, and you need all your faculties performing at 100 percent if you intend to survive to ride another day.*)

I'm sure there were more, but that's all I remember these days. I suppose I'm just lucky to have survived the 10 years or so it took me to slowly unlearn all those bits of wisdom. And to this day, I often feel a bit sorry for some riders I see actually following some of these practices, knowing that the truth is that this is what they were taught by their peers, and they probably just haven't had the opportunity or occasion to learn the truth yet.

Chapter 9
Miscellaneous Essentials

Attitude!

Among my varied endeavors these days, my favorite is leading organized motorcycle tours of my beloved Mojave Desert, following parts of old Route 66. And since the majority of my clients are Easterners who've never seen a desert before in their lives, for months in advance, I send out e-mails with all kinds of advice about what to expect, how to dress, how to pack, and so forth. ("All hotels either have a hairdryer in the room, or will loan you one. Tell your wife she really doesn't need to pack one on the bike!") But I think perhaps the most important advice I give is this: "Of all the things you want to remember to bring along on a motorcycle tour, the most essential of all is a good attitude."

Ultimately all you really need for motorcycle touring is a good bike and a sense of adventure.

After about 35 years of touring all over the planet, I firmly believe that a bad attitude can ruin the best of trips, and a good attitude can make even a ride fraught with adversity an adventure to be remembered and treasured. Perhaps even more crucial when dealing with groups of riders is that one person on the tour with a really bad attitude has the power to spoil the ride for everyone around them. I've seen it happen, and it's an ugly sight.

My personal favorite story of the power of a positive attitude takes place in a high Alpine pass. My good friend Marc and I had been riding since about 6:00 that morning, pretty much just going wherever the wind blew us. But as the afternoon got later, we started trying to figure out how to find our way to the hotel where we were supposed to meet up with our tour group that night. Before long, it became evident we had taken a wrong turn somewhere. As we reached the summit of what was, I believe, our fourth or fifth mountain pass that day, the sky turned dark and a freezing rain began falling. Most Alpine

The type of bike matters less than the desire to hit the road.

roads are very narrow to begin with, and this particular one was barely a single car width across, but eventually I spotted a narrow gravel shoulder and pulled over. As Marc pulled up behind me, I motioned him alongside and flipped up my faceshield. "Hey, Marc. Any idea where this road goes?"

He flipped up his own shield and stared at me for a moment before replying, "Nope. Not a clue."

"Well then," I said, "any chance you happen to know what country we're in?"

Again he hesitated before replying, "Now that you mention it—no, I'm not quite sure. At that last border crossing we entered Switzerland, but on these back roads we've been riding, I suppose we could have crossed into Austria sometime this afternoon . . . maybe even Italy."

"Then I don't suppose you know what direction our hotel is in?"

"No, but let me ask you a question."

"Shoot."

"Wasn't that a great road we just came up?"

"Fantastic," I replied. "In fact, the whole day's ride has been incredible. Indescribable."

"Well then," he said, a smile creeping across his face, "does any of the rest really matter?"

I thought about it for a second. We were lost in a foreign country, high in the mountains. It was getting dark, and the rain was turning to snow. I was wet and cold, but in fact, was having the ride of my life. So I said, "Now that you mention it, old friend—no, it really doesn't matter!"

"Well then," said my favorite riding buddy, "what are we sitting here for? Let's ride!"

As it turned out, we found a familiar name on a road sign about 30 clicks later, and within an hour actually found our way to the correct hotel, to the surprise of us both. Another hour and a hot shower later and we were settled in overstuffed chairs in an eighteenth-century gasthaus, quaffing steins of the local brew and munching on delicious little smoked sausages—the perfect end to a perfect day.

But as we sat there reflecting on how beautiful life can be, several other motorcyclists arrived, in small groups and singles. All, like Marc and I, revealed giant smiles as they pulled off their helmets outside the window of the gasthaus, even though they were obviously soaking wet and shivering. All, that is, except for one couple. The scowl on the woman's face wouldn't become visible until she pulled off her helmet, but even before that we could see trouble brewing by the way she jumped off the back of the bike, tore off her soggy gloves, and threw them violently on the ground. We couldn't hear anything through the window, but the husband's cringing body language as he backed away from her spoke volumes.

In a few minutes she came inside, leaving her partner to unpack the bike, scowled at everyone in the room, and planted herself in a far corner, evidently so as not to be infected with our laughter and revelry, as the rest of us shared stories of being lost, cold, and wet in the Alps. Quite frankly, I believe it angered her even more to see that we were making light of the very conditions that had ruined her vacation.

Later, I met and spoke with another couple who had been traveling with the sourpuss and her spouse, and they told of how she had found something to complain about every day of their journey, making not only herself miserable, but her husband and friends as well. This other couple was already making plans to get up extra early the next morning, and leaving a message for their friends that they had to leave for some made-up reason. The way they saw it, it was their only hope of salvaging some pleasure from their vacation. They felt sorry for the husband, but weren't about to continue having their good time ruined by his wife.

Attitude. Trust me. It's the single, most essential thing to remember to take along on your next ride, be it a day trip in the country, or a month crisscrossing Europe.

Attitude. Trust me. It's the single, most essential thing to remember to take along on your next ride, be it a day trip in the country, or a month crisscrossing Europe.

Don't leave home without it.

Patience

For nearly 30 years now, I've been participating in motorcycle tours all over the planet. Some of my travels have been as the guest of one motorcycle manufacturer or another, but most have been either as a paid client or as a tour leader or assistant tour leader. All in all, I suppose I've been on about 100 to 150 guided motorcycle tours. For the most part, I enjoy being a tour leader, even though it often entails being part babysitter, part traffic cop, part referee, and part psychologist. It's all part of the game, but one role I have to play that often comes close to driving me crazy is that of font of all knowledge.

Continued on page 219

Bob and Kaye's Excellent Adventure

The following is a true story (with a few minor embellishments).

Day One

The tour group was on its way to a seven-day ride through the national parks of Utah. At our first gas stop just outside of Pasadena, one of my assistant tour leaders came running over. "Bob just filled his bike with diesel," he proclaimed, "and now it won't run."

"Terrific," I thought, "What a great way to start the tour!"

We pushed the brand-new Gold Wing across the parking lot to place in the shade and pondered our next course of action. I was afraid this would mean leaving Bob and his wife behind with one of my helpers while we had a trailer bring out a new bike for him and take the stricken Wing back to L.A. But then I decided to call my buddy Mike, one of the owners of a Gold Wing shop, to ask for advice. "It's not such a big deal," Mike said. "Just siphon as much of the diesel out as you can, and fill the bike back up with premium gas. It will be hard to start, and will smoke and run like crap for a while, but even that will clear up after the first tank, and you'll be okay."

To make a long story short, we borrowed a siphon hose from a truck driver and bought six gallon jugs of water, which we promptly emptied so we could use them to store the diesel. Bob, being the one who pumped the diesel into the bike in the first place, was granted the honor of sucking on the rubber hose to get things started. I expected we would only get about five of the tank's 6.6 gallons out, but by taping the hose to a stick and jamming it all the way to the bottom of the tank, we actually removed a bit more than six gallons. After pushing the bike back to the pump and filling it with premium gasoline, we tried starting it. It took about a dozen tries, and I was beginning to worry the battery would give out before the engine caught, but eventually the big six-cylinder coughed and spit out a cloud of black smoke, and continued running. True to Mike's prediction, it ran a bit rough and smoked a lot for a few miles, but we were back on the road, having only lost about two hours.

Day Two

As we pulled into a rest stop on a mountain road, a relatively inexperienced rider at the back of the pack lost his footing while trying to park, and his bike toppled over. Bob immediately spotted this in his rearview, and being the good guy that he was, jumped off his own bike and rushed back to help. Unfortunately, in his haste he failed to notice that he'd parked his own bike on an incline, in neutral, and as he stepped away, it rolled off the kickstand

and toppled over, dumping his wife, Kaye, on the tarmac. Luckily she was unhurt, save a bruised shoulder, and neither bike was damaged beyond a few scratches, and we were back on our way within a few minutes.

Day Three

As we packed to leave in the morning, Kaye found that she had left some prescription medicine she needed in the previous night's hotel room, which was now over 400 miles away. A quick check with the hotel desk found us a clinic a few miles in the opposite direction of where we were headed. Unfortunately, it would not open until an hour after our planned departure, so I left one of my assistants behind to help the hapless couple catch up with us after seeing a doctor and getting a new prescription. As it was, Bob and Kaye were back with the group by lunch, though by now, the rest of the group was making a great show of not sitting or riding too close to Diesel Bob and Poor Kaye. (All in good fun, of course.)

Day Four

As we rolled out of the mountains and into the desert, the temperature began to climb, and rather than wait until the next stop, Kaye decided to wiggle out of her (brand-new, color-matched) insulated jacket while riding down the interstate. She managed it too, but as she tried to stow the jacket between herself and Bob, a strong gust of wind from the side caught it, lifting it up into the air, across the median, and directly under the wheels of an oncoming semi. That was the last we ever saw of it, and luckily she had nothing important in the pockets, but Bob had to loan her his own jacket for the remainder of the trip, and to suffer along wearing only his liner.

Day Five

As we were packing up in the morning, one of the other riders noticed that Bob had left his bike keys on the seat of his bike when he went back into the room for the rest of his bags, and quickly pocketed them, bringing them to me for a joke. I only let him suffer for about a minute before tossing him the lost keys. It just wasn't very funny anymore.

Day Six

We had all gassed up and were lined up waiting to leave the gas station parking lot while a couple of the folks used the restrooms. Bob decided

> ... as she tried to stow the jacket between herself and Bob, a strong gust of wind from the side caught it, lifting it up into the air, across the median, and directly under the wheels of an oncoming semi.

that he was a bit too close to the bike parked alongside him, and considering recent his run of bad luck, opted to back up a bit to give himself more clearance before pulling out. Unfortunately, my assistant had parked his BMW behind and just to the side of Bob's Wing, precisely in the blind spot where it didn't show up in the mirrors. As the GL's trunk caught the handlebar, the BMW twisted sideways and toppled over. The fairing and turn signal were broken, some deep gouges were left in the tank and cylinder head cover, but at least the bike was still usable. Bob, on the other hand, was starting to look a bit the worse for wear.

Day Seven

Despite her previous mishap with removing a jacket in flight, Kaye once again got a bit warm as we transitioned from mountains to desert, but this time, she opted to simply slip her arms out and leave the jacket pinned behind her, against the seat; seemingly a good plan, until her arm got caught. Though it seemed just one more good pull might free it up, instead she managed to dislocate her shoulder. Luckily, everything went back in place okay, but coupled with the previous shoulder injury from the fall, she could hardly move her arm at all now. Though we offered to get her to a doctor, we had a nurse along on the ride who fixed Kaye up with a sling from our first-aid kit, and she opted to finish out the ride. The only problems were that it took a bit of help to get her on and off the bike, and Bob had to get up a bit earlier in the morning to get her dressed.

It Is What You Make It

Problems are going happen on tours, particularly with large groups. It's all part of the game. In fact, on the last day of each tour we give out a tongue-in-cheek Hard Luck Award to the person or couple who had the most interesting mishap during the week. But Bob and Poor Kaye set a whole new standard. In fact, it was even worse than what I've written here. These were just the highlights. But there is an important moral to their story.

You see, despite everything, this couple was determined not to let anything ruin their vacation. No matter how many dark clouds followed them

> No matter how many dark clouds followed them around, or how many minor disasters tried to spoil their fun, they laughed and smiled their way through it all.

around, or how many minor disasters tried to spoil their fun, they laughed and smiled their way through it all. And though you might have thought their mishaps would have cast a pall over the entire tour, just the opposite happened. They laughed at themselves, and invited the rest of us to laugh along with them. And in doing so, they became the most enjoyable couple to be around, thereby ensuring that everyone had a good time.

I wish everyone I took on tour could be like them.

Continued from page 215

People on a tour to a strange place tend to ask lots of questions, so a tour guide really needs to know the area he's guiding folks through, and to prepare to answer all sorts of questions. Here again, though, that's something I enjoy—until the stupid questions start. Generally, in any group of a dozen or more riders, I find I'll have at least one who repeatedly badgers me with stupid questions. It makes me crazy. I should qualify that statement—it isn't actually the questions that make me nuts; it's my not being able to answer them the way I would really like to. Remember, I'm a writer by trade, and have been credited with having at least a moderately quick wit, which means I can usually come up with a pretty good, smart-ass answer to most dumb questions, but being a professional tour guide means I have to bite my tongue and give more reasoned responses.

So I've decided to share some of the stranger questions I've gotten over the years, and this time I can actually answer them the way I would have liked.

My most popular tour is my Route 66 Old West Adventure through the deserts of Southern California, Arizona, and Nevada. During these tours I've been asked:

If you're like me, regular life is just something you do until you can take your next trip.

- While viewing the incredible night sky of Death Valley: "Is that the same moon we see in New England?" (No, this is the southern moon. It's much larger and slightly more yellow.)

- Out in the Mojave Desert: "Which direction is north out here?" (Always to your left.)

- At the evening meeting, after explaining the different tours available the next morning: "What time does the nine o'clock tour leave?" (About 6:30, but if I'm not there, wait for me.)

- After stopping for entry passes to Death Valley: "How long is the one-day pass good for?" (Normally 17 hours, but 18 during daylight savings time.)

- On viewing the ruins of an ancient Indian village: "Why did the Indians build so many ruins?" (To confuse the Evil Spirits.)

- Standing on the south rim of the Grand Canyon: "How long did it take them to dig this?" (Almost 50 years—but remember, it was a government project.)

- On one of the tours where we offer luggage van service: "Should I put the luggage outside the door before or after I go to sleep?" (Before you go to sleep, but not after you wake up.)

- On arriving back at the California coastline, standing on the beach: "How far above sea level are we here?" (Just barely far enough.)

One of my favorite assistant tour guides, when he can get away to join us, is my friend Marc from Canada. On a recent tour with him, on the first day out, one of the ladies on the tour waited until we were apart, then rushed up to me and whispered in my ear, "I'd like to ask Marc something, but first I need to know if he speaks English or only Canadian?" (Actually, he's from southeastern Canada and is bilingual—he speaks Acadian and Portugese—but I can translate for you.)

I know this one is going to sound too ridiculous to be true, but I swear it happened. In fact, I had a T-shirt made to commemorate the event. Marc and

This was on the back of an 80-plus gentleman that toured with me for seven days and about 3,000 miles. At the end, he wasn't ready to quit, and he wasn't the oldest rider on the tour, either. Don't let anyone tell you you're too old to tour.

I had been touring through the Alps with a group, and after several days in Germany and Switzerland, when we arrived in Austria, a lady said, "I've been waiting for this. Now that we're in Austria I can't wait to see some kangaroos!" (My T-shirt says "Welcome to Austria," and has a "kangaroo crossing" road sign.)

That same lady, on our first day in Italy, asked: "Will I be able to speak English here?" (I doubt it, since you couldn't speak it before we arrived.)

My second-favorite question was also asked while I was on tour, but came from someone with an entirely different tour group. We had ridden for several days across Brazil to see the incredibly awesome Iguacu Falls, a set of waterfalls on the Parana River that's over three times the size of Niagara. The Brazilian government has built a series of walkways that allow you to walk out over the top of the falls, and as I was standing there gawking at the most amazing sight I had ever seen, with billions of gallons of water pouring over a precipice nearly eight miles wide, I heard a lady with a British accent in the tour group standing near me say to her tour guide, "We were thinking of coming back to see it at night, but were wondering, what time do they turn off the falls?" (10 p.m. on weekdays, but they keep them running until midnight on weekends and holidays.)

Now for my all-time favorite, even though it isn't exactly a question. I'd been asked to lead a group of six motorcycle journalists from Russia on a loop from Las Vegas to Hoover Dam, and around through the Valley of Fire State Park. Five of the Russians spoke virtually no English at all, but one, named Salvatov, had a rudimentary understanding of the language, so he acted as translator. Things went just fine at Hoover Dam, and around the lake at the entrance to the Valley of Fire. I stopped the group there, and explained to Salvatov that I was going to ride ahead to a particularly good photo vantage point I knew of, to set up my camera. He was to follow with the group in about 15 minutes, and I would get some great photos for them to take home, with all of them riding through the crimson canyons. I was pretty sure he understood, so I took off, found my spot about two miles down the road, set up my camera, and waited. And waited. After half an hour had gone by, I packed up the camera and starting riding back. About a mile down the road, there were the six Russians, their bikes pulled off the road, milling about. I pulled over, jumped off my bike, pulled off my helmet and walked up to Salvatov. "What's wrong? I asked. "Why are you stopped here?" To which he silently replied by simply pointing to the black-and-white highway sign just in front of their bikes.

It said, "No Passing." So they didn't.

When you're traveling with a large group, make certain that your riding partners have the proper training.

In Conclusion

Well, I'd like to say, "That's it," but it really isn't, by any means. I hope you've come to realize after reading this that this is only a primer, or a starting point for launching your touring adventure. And hopefully, even for those seasoned touring riders, it has in some small way expanded their knowledge of our favorite sport. But in reality, we all know there is much, much more to learn, and the learning never stops. After about 40 years and well over one million miles of touring, I find I'm still learning new things almost every week, all of which in some way add to the experience.

Far beyond anything this book can teach you, the actual touring experience, and particularly the other riders with whom you'll interact, will teach you much more. The experts call it "experiential learning," and it's where probably three-quarters of my own knowledge on the subject comes from. Practically everyone you meet along the way will have some small tidbit of knowledge to impart, so I encourage you to talk to them at rallies, club meetings, or just casual encounters alongside the road. And in return, you might have something to share with them, hopefully something you've learned from this book.

If that happens, then my job is done.

Ride long, and ride safe.

— *Fred Rau*

Whether you're riding across the county or across the planet, it's all good.

Index